Further Scenes of Shalford Past

Margaret Dierden

**A third collection of pieces on the history
of Shalford in Surrey**

2009

© Margaret Dierden 2009

By the same author
Scenes of Shalford Past 2002
More Scenes of Shalford Past 2006

Shalford School 1855-2005, 150 Years of a Village School, 2005

Most of these pieces first appeared in the Shalford parish magazine

Cover photograph: 38 and 36 The Street in 1916 from the Surrey Photographic Survey
(reproduced courtesy of Surrey History Centre)

Published by Margaret Dierden 15 Tilehouse Road Guildford Surrey GU4 8AP
2009

Contents

Water Works

Water or Heritage? That was the choice confronting the local authorities in the early 1960s, faced with having to decide whether to allow the demolition of Shalford House - a Grade II* listed building - to make way for a new water extraction and treatment works.

Shalford House was the mansion house of the Austen, later Godwin-Austen, family who by the mid-nineteenth century were the major landowners in Shalford. Brothers George and John Austen bought the Rectory Manor lands from Sir George More of Loseley in 1599 and in 1608 built a new house behind the church. This timber-framed Jacobean house was extended and refronted in the eighteenth century, with a third storey added. For much of the nineteenth century the house was let to tenants. But when Robert Alfred Cloyne Godwin-Austen inherited the property in 1872 he moved across from Chilworth Manor with his large family and installed them in the family seat. Robert Godwin-Austen was a highly-regarded Fellow of the Geological Society and published many articles in scientific journals; his son Henry Haversham Godwin-Austen, who moved to Shalford House after his father's death in 1884, was an explorer and mountaineer who had spent twenty years surveying and mapping northern India. The second highest peak of the Himalayas, K2, was originally named Mount Godwin-Austen in his honour. He published over 130 scientific articles as well as his magisterial *Land and Freshwater Molluscs of India* and *Fauna of British India*. In 1899 he moved from Shalford House to another family property at Nore near Hascombe. Shalford House was let again.

The house then became briefly a boys' prep school, then a hotel – the Shalford Park Hotel - for twenty five years. Just before the war it was sold to Guildford Borough Council. Cornhill Insurance took it on a non-repairing lease at the beginning of the war. When the lease expired in 1956 the house was in a very bad state; it might have been demolished then but gained a few more years respite as a furniture store. The problem lay

Shalford House in its heyday, in 1837

Shalford House in 1962 (photographed by K Gravett. Reproduced by permission of English Heritage NMR)
Robert Alfred Cloyne Godwin-Austen's grave is the cross to the left

in the attitude towards old buildings at that time – no–one wanted the expense of restoring the house and no-one wanted to use it. According to Surrey County Council's folders of correspondence and minutes on the subject, even Major Robert Godwin-Austen (son of Henry Haversham) seemed to accept the idea of demolition rather than have the house crumble away. Ideally, though, he would have liked to see it as a museum.

By the mid 1960s the site had caught the attention of the Guildford and Godalming District Water Board, whose difficulties in securing a reliable supply were creating headlines such as 'What Happened to all the Water?' and provoking angry letters to the newspapers. Shalford was pinpointed because here the dirty waters of the Wey were diluted by the cleaner Cranleigh Water (the southern branch of the Wey) and the Tillingbourne. The confluence of the Tillingbourne and the Wey beside Shalford House seemed by far the most suitable location for water extraction.

The Tillingbourne was particularly clean and fast-flowing; its 5 million gallons per day flow was more than enough to meet demand, and would only be supplemented from the much dirtier Wey if necessary. To save Shalford House it would have been possible to locate the treatment works somewhere else and pump along the water from the intake.

Alternative sites included one in Shalford Park beside Shalford Road, about where the sports field car park and changing rooms are now, another on fields at the end of Tilehouse Road, and yet another on East Shalford Lane beyond Tilehouse Farm. But all these would be visually obtrusive in an area of natural beauty and be much more costly to operate. The Shalford House site was chosen for the works because it was the least obtrusive and the most efficient to operate. In 1967, despite objections, the house was demolished.

Today, forty years on, water is no longer supplied by a small local board but instead by Thames Water, a giant company owned by an Australian bank. The works are impressive, upgraded over the last few years. The change of ownership has little impact on day-to-day operations: stringent regulations issued by the Drinking Water Inspectorate cover all aspects of all materials coming into contact with the water. Security has increased; the site used to be open and people would wander in and picnic on the banks of the Tillingbourne. The wire fence now closing off the site has brought some advantages for wildlife: the undisturbed area by the water intakes is peaceful and wild, almost a nature reserve, with herons and water fowl among the flag irises. A wildlife group has built an otters' holt on the riverbank, and terrapins live in a quiet side channel.

On average 190,000 litres of water per second flow into the site, equivalent to 16.4 million litres, or 3.4 million gallons per day. The proportions taken from the Tillingbourne and the Wey are now about 50/50, although either river can meet full demand. In an emergency – such as a pollution incident – the intakes can be closed off. Improvements in technology over the last few years mean that dirty water can now be cleaned more efficiently. The Wey is in fact much cleaner than it was forty years ago, although it flows through more built-up areas with busy roads than does the Tillingbourne and therefore receives more pollution from surface run-off.

A system of channels, tanks and filters takes the water through the works. Monitored for levels of pollutants, physically and chemically cleansed, filtered and micro-filtered, the water takes about 6-12 hours to pass from the intakes to the point where it leaves the works, pumped to reservoirs at Pewley Hill, The Mount, Frith Hill and Munstead. Shalford supplies about 105,000 people in Guildford and Godalming with water. It is the largest of six treatment works in a network with 14 reservoirs. The treatment works are designed to cover for each other in an emergency and a kind of grid system operates to supply water to other areas if necessary. Shalford could even supply water to Haslemere.

So, Water or Heritage? Is the waterworks worth the loss of Shalford House? The grouping of village, church and mansion house was of historic importance – interdependent for centuries, none makes complete sense without the others. And it is hard to imagine that Shalford House would not have been saved had it managed to hang on for a few more years. By now it could have been a hotel again, a conference centre, or luxury apartments. On the other hand, despite advances in technology, a water treatment works located some distance from the intakes would be costly and less efficient as well as visually obtrusive. As they are, the works are tucked away behind the churchyard; most people passing through the village are unaware of their presence.

And at the heart of it all is the little river Tillingbourne – the reason for Shalford's existence in the first place – cleaner now than a few centuries ago when village industries crowded its banks. It is still playing its role at the heart of the community, now by supplying clean water to an even wider area. Guildford residents are lucky to get their water from the Shalford works. Its filters are world class with an international reputation. The water is full of health-giving minerals – a characteristic of chalky areas. Never buy bottled water – the water from our own rivers is so much better.

With many thanks to Thames Water for a tour of the works.

Sources
Documents relating to the demolition of Shalford House and the construction of the water treatment works ref CC/512/27 at Surrey History Centre.
1837 drawing of Shalford House ref G111/9/29/2 reproduced by kind permission of Surrey History Centre and Lt Col R H Godwin-Austen DL.

Shalford Water Treatment Works (May 2008)
The cycle path in the foreground was the carriage drive from Shalford House
leading through Shalford Park to the main road

'The Shop'

People still call it 'the shop', even though it closed over twenty years ago. And Claude Lofting is still remembered and missed – especially by villagers who have to get into their cars and drive to find a loaf and bread or a pint of milk.

This house with its two yellow doors (the two on the left in the picture below, also see front cover) is now 38 The Street, but was previously numbered as 1 The Street. It was a grocer's shop from at least the 1840s and for many years Shalford's Post Office. From the early 1900s it also housed a café. Claude, the last shopkeeper, had to close the shop through ill-health in 1987 but stayed there until his death in 1996. He loved his home with all its ancient features. The word 'houseproud' might have been invented for Claude. No-one is likely to forget the sight of his tiny figure perched on a stepladder, brush in hand, painting his doors and windows just inches from heavy lorries thundering by.

His grandfather came from Walton-on-Thames in the early 1920s to take over the premises. A postcard of the time shows the familiar frontage with a hanging sign 'Tocos Chintz Tea Shoppe.' The reverse apparently proclaimed the availability of 'coffee, lunches, teas and dinners.' Claude became the third generation of his family to live in the house when he came to help his parents run the shop after the war. He repainted the sign to read 'Lofting's Chintz Tea Rooms.' The door on the far left led into the café. They had to brick up the door inside after they found too many people using it to exit without paying for their tea. When Claude became sole proprietor in the late 1950s the tea rooms were closed down, but he kept the shop open for cigarettes, confectionery and groceries. People still remember the café: it was a favourite haunt of employees of Cornhill Insurance, which occupied Shalford House during and just after the war.

Ronald Rooke, or 'Rookie,' living just along the road in The Old Studio, got on famously with Claude. The fact that he was open all hours and always had what you

wanted, as well as his many kindnesses, led Rookie to joke that Claude deserved a knighthood. Rookie immortalised Claude in one of his caricatures. When it was finished he took it along to the shop, made Claude kneel down, and knighted him with his walking stick. Claude was very proud of the picture and it hung on the wall until his death.

Claude was initially a reluctant shopkeeper, considering it his duty to help his parents but secretly yearning for tailoring, his original calling. He kept up the skill and his perfectly tailored clothes were his own work. He knew about his family's Dutch origins and about his ancestor, merchant and inventor John Lofting, who patented a machine for dimpling thimbles in 1693.

Claude Lofting by 'Rookie' (courtesy of Jean Rooke)

But Claude never knew about the tailors who lived in his house in Elizabethan times. Although the present building is dated to the early seventeenth century, that row of cottages has been there since the Middle Ages, much rebuilt, extended and divided. In the sixteenth century the house was known as Fletchers. When tailor John Beckes died in 1587 he left it to his sons Robert and William. Robert was also a tailor: his will in 1598 mentions his 'chest, shop board, shears, pressing iron and other tailoring implements.' With the country prepared to face a Spanish invasion as the Armada approached the able-bodied men of the village were summoned to arms: Robert and William Beckes appear on the muster roll as pikemen.

Like the other cottages in the row Fletchers was at first home to village craftsmen and small husbandmen farming a few acres of land nearby. The cottage next door, the Corner House (now Beech House) on the corner of Dagley Lane, became gentrified in the seventeenth century and in 1637 took a piece of Fletchers' garden. The remaining houses in the row became much subdivided and extended over the years and by Victorian times were largely occupied by labourers, gardeners and servants on the Godwin-Austen estate.

By 1890 the village was losing out to the new economic and social centre around the Common, and the Post Office moved down to Station Road, then Kings Road. As car ownership increased in the early twentieth century the new café in The Street took advantage of passing trade. But traffic has become the village's curse, and cars and supermarkets have killed off the little shops. Today, not only is there no shop in the old village, but all the grocers' shops in Station Road and Kings Road have gone as well. Claude was a rarity even twenty years ago, and now 'the shop' is just a folk memory.

Sources: Records of Shalford Rectory Manor at Surrey History Centre G111/2/1&2; *Surrey Musters Vols. I, II, & IV* Surrey Record Society Vols. **III** and **X;** Robert Bax (Beckes)'s will 1598. Archdeaconry of Surrey DW/PA/7/7 f 206, London Metropolitan Archives. Interview with Claude Lofting in 1993.

The Stocks

The old photograph below shows the village stocks outside the church gate. These are not quite the stocks we see today: in 1951 they were rebuilt by a parishioner, who replaced most of the rotten old wood. Now the stocks are prized as part of the village's heritage, but it was not always so, as shown by a letter printed in the *Surrey Advertiser* on 1 February 1868:

> Sir – I beg to draw your attention to a great eyesore existing in this parish, in the shape of the old stocks – though not quite complete – which stand just outside our pretty churchyard, and are to be seen by everyone passing. This remnant of a bye-gone age appears to stand as a monument of disgrace to the parishioners…The services of the stocks are no longer required. We have now, however, an inspector of nuisances and I hope he will see to this matter, and bring the subject before the authorities in such a manner that an order may be granted for the removal of the abomination and the woodwork given to some poor widow for firing.
> Yours etc. A Constant Reader, Shalford

The village stocks outside the churchyard photographed in 1916 (Surrey Photographic Survey, reproduced courtesy of Surrey History Centre)

What Lies Beneath

A hidden landscape of old tracks and fields lies beneath the modern world. Once at the heart of the community many of these are now obscure or forgotten, overtaken by modern development and modern communications

Opposite the Parrot a footpath across the Common marks the old route from Broadford towards Dagley Lane. Another branch led to the main road by the Scout Hut.

Take that awkward bend on Broadford Road near the Parrot. The stretch of wide straight road across the Common to the A281 is quite new in historical terms, dating from the early nineteenth century. The original route turned north from Broadford, with one branch joining the main road and another leading into Dagley Lane, emerging in The Street between the Seahorse and Beech House.

Dagley (sometimes Dagden or Dagwell) Lane was a direct route from Broadford to Shalford village and Guildford. In the Middle Ages some of the villagers - those living on land belonging to Braboeuf Manor - would have driven their animals along it to feed on Braboeuf's Common at Broadford. Much later Dagley Lane served as a rear entrance to Shalford House, and in 1815 a little Regency lodge was built there (since demolished). Now the lane is enjoying a new lease of life as part of the cycle path between Guildford and Godalming.

Parsonage Lane, closed and overgrown. In the distance is Bridge House/The Old Vicarage on the main road north of the church

Parsonage Lane was closed when Tilehouse Road was built in the 1950s, although it hadn't been used by wheeled traffic for some considerable time. It forked from the main road opposite the Old

Vicarage/Bridge House. The banks of the lane are still visible through the trees (but please don't take your eyes off the road on that dangerous bend). The beginning of the Tilehouse Road cul-de-sac is built along the upper part of Parsonage Lane, but the old lane is soon hidden in the field, plunging amid the nettles and brambles of its overgrown hedges towards the fence separating it from the main road. Parsonage Lane was an ancient route leading from East Shalford Lane towards the river crossing at St Catherine's, and was probably older than the village. The earliest map of the village, drawn for George Austen around 1600, shows fields with Saxon names – Debnershe and Homehawes - either side of Parsonage Lane, suggesting that the lane existed before the farmland was laid out. In later times this lane provided a route into Guildford avoiding two fords across the Tillingbourne.

Pilgrims Way (forget the pilgrims, this is just Victorian romancing) was closed off from the main road by a gate – Shalford Hatch – to stop animals grazing in the open or common fields from straying. Animals were turned out onto the fields after harvest – notice to do so was given by the Rectory Manor's bailiff - to manure the land for the next year's crops. The route of Pilgrims Way and Echo Pit Road separated Shalford's Upper and Lower Common Fields, where medieval villagers cultivated their acre and half acre strips. The trackway led to Merrow via Northdown Lane and Pewley Down; when it reached Merrow it was called Shalford Lane.

Pilgrims Way is a more alluring name than its earlier one - Crapitts Lane. Six acres of land called 'The Crapitts,' or 'Crapetts', lay beside what is now the junction of Pilgrims Way and Echo Pit Road. In 1610 George Austen paid for 'casting the pond at Crapitts', in other words clearing out the mud. The pond is still there, very overgrown, on the far side of the top track leading from the Chantries car park. A little house at Crapitts and its quarter acre of garden disappeared when the hop garden at Crapitts was extended in the seventeenth century. By the late eighteenth century Crapitts had been absorbed into the Austens' eleven-acre Great Hop Garden Field. The original meaning of Crapitts could be crab apple trees, or, just maybe, land where the dyeplant madder was grown (from the Old English word for madder. This possibility is interesting in view of Guildford's medieval cloth industry).

Other now-forgotten place-names are marked on George Austen's map. On the side of the hill next to Crapitts lay an area called Maynesbury, which had become part of the Common Fields. The name seems Saxon in origin and must relate to a phase of agriculture and settlement earlier than the Common Fields and therefore earlier than the village itself. Nearby, an area called The Nyes refers to land brought into cultivation in the Middle Ages, when rapidly increasing population put pressure on land and resources. Both Crapitts and The Nyes were part of a system of small fields and closes that operated alongside the open Common Fields.

Footpaths crossed the fields and survived the agricultural reorganisation of the nineteenth century and the building development of the twentieth. Now they run between garden fences on Chantry View Road. Warwicks Bench Road, the link between Echo Pit Road and Warwicks Bench that now provides a back route into Guildford, dates only from the late 1890s - hence the steep bends at either end where it joins roads that were once ancient routes. Warwicks Bench and South Hill follow the line of one of these footpaths across the fields into Guildford. Warwicks Bench and Velvet Walk nearby were favourite haunts for people taking a stroll out of Guildford in the eighteenth century (such walks are mentioned in antiquarian William Bray's journal in the 1750s).

Beyond the Common Fields lay Halfway House Farm, part of which was the great chalk pit. It became part of the Austen estate in 1808 and was renamed Chalk Pit Farm. The ancient farmhouse – Halfway Grange - remains at the end of Chantry View Road, the name having reverted to its historic roots.

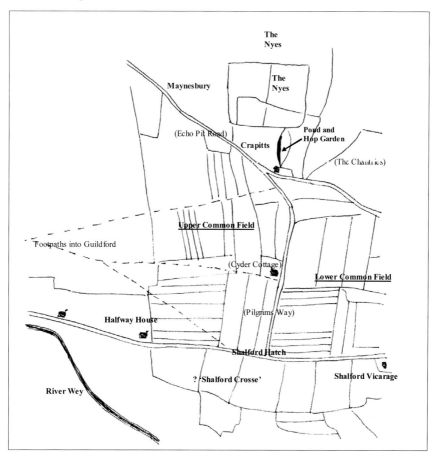

The Pilgrims Way area, based on George Austen's map of Shalford made in the early 1600s and other documents relating to the Common Fields

At the bottom of Pilgrims Way in the region of Shalford Park was an area known as 'Shalford Crosse', mentioned in two documents from 1511 and 1625, which suggests that the name was of long-standing. This is the presumed location of Shalford's medieval fair. Could Shalford Cross refer to a preaching cross or market cross erected for the fair and remaining in folk memory? The fair itself may not have survived the Middle Ages. Or is this simply a reference to cross roads – where the track from Merrow met the main road from Guildford, and a footpath then crossed the glebeland towards the river at St Catherine's (where there was a footbridge until around 1608, then a ferry)?

Tilehouse Farm in East Shalford Lane developed on the site of Shalford's medieval tile industry and was a holding under Shalford Rectory Manor

Close to the village Tilehouse Farm still exists as a reminder of Shalford's tile industry of 700 years ago. Tile production in Shalford continued for at least a century in the 1300s – 1400s. On several occasions the tiles were transported to the Bishop of Winchester's castle in Farnham – an expensive journey for such heavy goods. There must have been a closer market for the tiles to keep the industry in business for so long – Guildford town and castle are the obvious candidates. George Austen's map from the early 1600s, long after the industry had finished, shows two plots at Tilehouse Farm: 'Tylost' where the kiln must have stood (*ost*=oast=kiln), and 'Tylland' nearer the river, where perhaps clay was extracted and other manufacturing processes carried out. Interestingly, a tile kiln of medieval design was discovered on the former 'Tylost' in 2008 during barn renovation work.

The steep pathway from Pilgrims Way to the corner of Warwicks Bench Road is part of an old footpath across the Common Fields into Guildford

Shalford's crowning glory is the Chantries – the tree-covered ridge overlooking the northern end of the parish. The name originally belonged to an area of woodland dedicated to the support of the Norbrigge Chantry in Guildford's Holy Trinity Church. This type of bequest was common in the later Middle Ages. The income supported a priest to pray for the soul of the deceased, which would reduce the length of time spent in Purgatory. The area of woodland was extended as a result of eighteenth and nineteenth century planting. Before this the northern slopes of the Chantries and St Martha's were given over to rabbit warrens. The warrener's house stood beside the bridleway leading towards Tyting, just west of South Warren Farm, which used to be known as Chantry or Tyting Warren. In 1618 Edward Bone and Edward Roker, warreners of Shalford, were indicted for murder, accused of stabbing to death John Blundell at the appropriately-named Deadman's Bush. (Roker fled, and Bone was found not guilty.)

Chinthurst Lane was the main road to Wonersh before Kings Road was developed. Until the railway arrived in 1849 Chinthurst Lane forked from the main road just in front of what is now Station Row. The stretch of road in front of Station Row and the Queen Victoria is in fact the top end of Chinthurst Lane. Chinthurst Hill marks the southern boundary of the parish. The *'-hurst'* element usually means a wooded hill, but can also refer to coppiced woods. Both interpretations suit Chinthurst Hill, much of which was covered with coppices for centuries. The will of Christian Baker, a widow who lived at 'Chinters' and died in 1619, reveals that she leased land on the hill on which she grew rye and beans; she also had a coppice there. Christian Baker's house, according to her father's will (Robert Stanlack, who died in 1603) had a piece of hill ground behind it to the south east. Perhaps she lived at Hill Cottage or possibly Chinthurst Farm. To leave a will at all meant that she was among the better-off inhabitants of Shalford: the total value of her worldly goods, including the growing rye and beans, 'hir aparell & the mony in hir purse' amounted to £9 19s 6d.

The name of Christmas Hill, or Christmas Hills, is a medieval survival. Possibly Christmas was the name of a family who once owned that 12 acres of land. Christmas has occurred locally as a surname, and property names in this area were often derived from a medieval owner. By the mid 1500s the parish church received a yearly payment, or church rent, from Christmas Hills: 2lb of wax, or 12d a year. In pre-Reformation times payments to the church often took the form of wax for the candles. After the Reformation this 12d per annum was still paid to the churchwardens towards the maintenance costs of the church. Recently the postal address 'Christmas Hill' has engulfed an area including Bradstone Brook, which strictly speaking is in East Shalford (an address the Royal Mail has forgotten). Christmas Hill proper is the low eminence on which the Village Hall stands; there were two fields – Upper and Lower Christmas Hill, both now built over. The Village Hall stands on Lower Christmas Hill. Part of the field boundary of Upper Christmas Hill can still be seen beside a footpath leading from Chinthurst Lane by Field Gate House.

Pound Place is another reminder of medieval agriculture. The houses overlook the site of a pound on the edge of the Common. Animals caught straying were impounded by the manorial bailiff and released on payment of a fine to the lord of the manor. This pound and this part of the Common belonged to the East Shalford manors of Shalford Clifford and Shalford Bradston. Shalford had three other pounds: Bramley Manor's pound stood in front of the Kiln Field (now occupied by Shalford Cemetery); Braboeuf Manor had a pound at Gosden Common, and Shalford Rectory Manor's pound was opposite the end of Pilgrims Way, on the glebeland near Park Cottages. The fields of Shalford Park were known in the eighteenth century as Hither and Further Pound Fields.

Many quirky and descriptive field names did not survive the agricultural reorganisations of the eighteenth and nineteenth centuries that went on in all parts of the parish. So where were Great Fagstars, the Long Fagstar, and the Little Fagstar, leased by Sir William More of Loseley to Thomas Parson of Gosdens in 1577? These fields were somewhere near Gosden House; the names - possibly indicating poor or marshy land – had disappeared by the time of the Tithe Map in 1842. Other unpromising land had escaped reorganisation: The Moats near Chinthurst Hill, The Drodges and Romping or Ramping Downs on the west side of Chinthurst Lane, and Sorrow Field – a typical name for less productive land – part of Summersbury Farm, all appear on the Tithe Map. Lower Boggeley by the Tillingbourne did not belie its name despite undergoing drainage work in the 1820s. At the northern foot of the Chantries Warrenhouse Field and Little Barracks were reminders of the former rabbit warren. Nearby a glade previously called Tinkers Bottom had changed to Tinklers Bottom, perhaps through confusion with William Tinkler, the gunpowder maker at Chilworth.

The medieval open fields and many small hedged enclosures were reorganised into larger fields in the eighteenth and nineteenth centuries; many of these have now disappeared under houses and gardens. The remainder have been adapted to suit modern farming needs. Likewise some old roads have been widened and strengthened for cars and lorries while others are now simply footpaths and bridleways. Roads, paths and trackways are the oldest man-made elements in the landscape and persist while all around them changes. Ancient routes thread through a hidden landscape formed and named by agriculture, village industry, and the church – the institutions around which life revolved - evidence of Shalford's development from the earliest times to the present day.

Main Sources
Shalford Tithe Map and Award, 1842 and 1845 at Surrey History Centre; map of Shalford c.1600 SHC ref G111/2/3; 'pond at Crapetts' in building accounts for Shalford House 1608-10, G1514/2; Shalford Rectory Manor rolls G111/2/1&2; 'Shalford Crosse' mentioned in LM 306 (also 'the crapetts') and G43/129; deeds of Halfway Farm G111/22; murderous warreners in Calendar of Assizes James I, Surrey Indictments, HMSO; mention of the Shalford tile industry in the Pipe Rolls of the Bishop of Winchester quoted in Nicholas Riall, *A Medieval Tile Kiln in Farnham Park*, Sy AC **84**, 1997 pp.145-146; list of Church Rents G43/281; will and inventory of Christian Baker 1619, Hampshire Record Office ref 1619/B03/1&2; Robert Stanlack's will 1603 DW/PA/7/7 f445 at London Metropolitan Archives; extracts from William Bray's diary *Sy AC* Vol **XLVI**; *The Landscape of Place Names*, Margaret Gelling and Ann Cole, 2000; *English Field Names* by John Field, 1972

Conan Doyle and the Twisted Man of Shalford

A fuss about Sir Arthur Conan Doyle's house at Hindhead brought to mind a story of his set in Shalford and published just over a century ago in 1906. The Culture Secretary recently refused to raise the listed status of his home, Undershaw, on the grounds that Conan Doyle was not a writer of the stature of, say, Jane Austen or Charles Dickens. Tell that to the millions of Sherlock Holmes fans worldwide.

Conan Doyle built Undershaw in 1897 and lived there for ten years. It was where he wrote some of his best work, resurrecting Sherlock Holmes after killing him off at the Reichenbach Falls, and producing perhaps the most filmed of all Holmes stories, *The Hound of the Baskervilles*. It is one of fate's little ironies that Conan Doyle detested Sherlock Holmes, to whom he owes his immortality, and considered his best work to be his historical novels, which are scarcely read now.

Of these he was most proud of *Sir Nigel*, published in 1906 and set in 1350 just after the Black Death and during the Hundred Years War. Nigel Loring was the poor but proud squire of Tilford, and the book deals with his early life before he set off for France to win honour and glory in the wars. One of his adventures involved rescuing the beautiful but wilful daughter of a neighbour from the clutches of Paul de la Fosse, the Twisted Man of Shalford, a malignant crippled figure inexplicably attractive to women. (It seems that Conan Doyle, a keen motorist, chose Shalford as the domain of this evil character in revenge for being caught speeding on the Portsmouth Road at Peasmarsh shortly before writing the book.) Conan Doyle studiously researched the fourteenth century world – the august Mary Renault commended his work – so one could argue that his (nowadays very non-PC) depiction of the twisted man reflected medieval attitudes as much as those of the early twentieth century. Altered social perceptions may explain why the novel went out of fashion. It was hugely popular when published and remained widely read until the 1940s.

It isn't just the twisted man. The attitudes to women and the glorification of war are difficult to relate to nowadays. Is this simply an expression of medieval chivalry or does it reflect Doyle himself: 'to his pure and knightly soul…every woman sat high and aloof, enthroned and exalted…far above the rude world of man.' And, 'what a woman loves in man is not his gross body, but rather his soul, his honour, his fame, the deeds with which he has made his life beautiful. Therefore you are winning love as well as glory when you turn to the wars.' This isn't just about the Middle Ages but reflects the Victorian idealisation of women. And can we see in Nigel's blithe departure to earn glory in France a premonition of those many thousands leaving for the western front in a blizzard of patriotic flag-waving only eight years after the book was published?

However, we are short on novels set in this area and Nigel's early adventures have plenty of local colour. Conan Doyle evidently spent some of his time at Hindhead in exploring the landscape of this part of Surrey. Edward III goes hawking on Crooksbury Heath; Nigel defends the bridge at Tilford in a feat of arms, comes to blows with outlaws at Puttenham and bargains with merchants outside busy Guildford Castle. He plights his troth to his lady-love at St Catherine's Chapel above 'the winding Wey', and his enduring memory of England is the sight of her straining to see him as he mounts through the 'dark Chantry woods' on the journey towards Kent and France. Approaching St Martha's he has another encounter with the twisted man of Shalford, whose retainers he fights off. Conan Doyle, like others of his time, was fascinated by the ideas of the Pilgrims' Way (now discredited) and the Old Road to the Kentish coast.

Perhaps Doyle's grip on local history was not quite as sure as on other aspects of the fourteenth century. When travelling to Shalford to confront the twisted man Nigel passes through Godalming and crosses the Peasmarsh: I don't know why he would choose the muddy and boggy approaches to the broad ford there when he only had to turn past Tilthams towards a perfectly good bridge at Unstead. Crossing Shalford Meadows (or does he mean the Common?) he sees on the dark hillside the red lights of Paul de la Fosse's house ('a den of profligacy and vice. No woman could cross the threshold and depart unstained.'). This is elsewhere named as Shalford Manor. If he meant a house standing where Manor Farm is now, on East Shalford Lane, I am not sure that it would have been visible from the Common even in the Middle Ages with no buildings in the way. And in fact the medieval manor was sited much lower, further along the lane, by the Tillingbourne (near the level crossing). Perhaps this is just artistic license; Doyle also invented a Shalford Nunnery, to which Nigel's love vows to commit herself should he fall in the wars.

Conan Doyle evidently found the Chantry woods romantic, a dark brooding presence in the landscape, and mentions them several times. Unfortunately Nigel lived over a century too early: the Norbrigge Chantry in Guildford's Holy Trinity Church which gave the woods their name was not founded until 1486. There was some woodland on the hill before that, but much less extensive than when Conan Doyle was writing. Most of the trees were planted in the eighteenth and nineteenth centuries, but pictures from the Godwin-Austen archive show smooth bare hilltops even in the 1840s.

It's rather unfair to criticise a novelist for refusing to let the facts get in the way of a good story. If you like knight errantry, pure maidens and noble squires, horse harness jangling through green leafy Surrey and bloody medieval warfare then you might find *Sir Nigel* a good read. Given Conan Doyle's reputation and the book's early popularity I'm surprised it hasn't been filmed – there are some good characters and with a bit of tweaking for modern sensibilities it might make a very watchable film or TV programme. Alas, Shalford wouldn't be a suitable location – too much recent development and far, far too much traffic.

Sir Nigel by Sir Arthur Conan Doyle, 1906, republished 1975 by John Murray and Jonathan Cape with an introduction by Mary Renault; republished by Wordsworth Classics 1994.
Sir Arthur Conan Doyle fined for speeding: *Surrey Advertiser* 5 June 1905.

Memories of Victorian Shalford

Shalford Women's Institute's scrapbook from 1950 contains the early memories of Sarah Elizabeth (Bessie) Hibberd who was then living at 2 The Street (now no. 36). She was born in Wiltshire in 1862 and lived in Shalford from the age of seven, attending the village school. She went on to teach there from 1876 to 1909:

'One of the things I remember most vividly were the treats given each summer to the school children; one year by Robert Austen of Shalford House, and the next by Mr Renton at Bradstone Brook. We had tea in the open, sitting on the ground (in the Monks' Walk at Shalford House) and what a good tea it was. There were two sorts of cake, bread and butter, and buns brought round in clothes-baskets. Afterwards there would be races and prizes for the boys and girls. At Christmas there was another treat – the Vicar gave us tea in the school.

On Sundays the church was always full, and on Harvest Festivals we had to put benches in the aisles. On Sunday morning the children assembled at the school and the Vicar took a class. Then we walked in twos to the Church for the service. Each Sunday we had to learn the Collect and the Gospel, and it was hard work at Easter with Good Friday's to learn as well. When I became a teacher I had to sign a five years contract, and this meant teaching every Sunday in the Sunday School as well.

Bessie Hibberd in a school staff photo from the 1890s

We always had to make an obeisance to the gentry of the village; the boys a bow and the girls a curtsey. I remember once getting into great trouble over this. We were walking up Quarry Hill one day when Miss Blagrave of Debnershe came along in her gig, and as we did not curtsey she reported us to the Vicar.

This road to Guildford was very dusty and the path high above the road. We would pass the lucky stone by the Vicarage and go through the tollgate at the end of Pilgrims Way. There was one small gate for pedestrians and a larger one for vehicles. The owner of the Malthouse, Mr Boxall, used to drive from Guildford each day in a small cart, wearing a plaid shawl round his shoulders and a high hat. We children laughed at him.

The Post Office was at No 1 the Street, and there was a letter box where the entrance to the Chintz Tea Room now is. When we first came to Shalford we lived at Christmas Hill. Of course all the water was drawn up from wells, and I remember one year when there was a drought and all the wells dried up and we had to fetch every drop from a spring up the lane.'

Courtesy of Shalford W.I., recorded by their President, Margaret Scott, c.1950.
Miss Hibberd died at the age of 100 in 1963.
Photograph courtesy of her great-niece Mrs Dorothy Baxell

The Toll-gate

The plaid shawl stands out in this old faded picture, and the craggy features of the keeper of Shalford Gate. Is the little family group the subject of the photograph or the table of tolls payable at the gate? The plaid shawl was a popular garment at the time (see previous chapter, *Memories of Victorian Shalford*, where Bessie Hibberd recalls Jesse Boxall of the Star Brewery wearing a plaid shawl as he drove his horse and cart each day from Guildford to Shalford during her 1870s childhood).

The toll-gate cottage stood on the main road, on the northern corner of Pilgrims Way (opposite the modern house called Toll Gate House). The days are long gone when you might bring a drove of cows or oxen along the road, paying 7d at the toll gate, or a drove of hogs, pigs, calves or lambs at the cost of 2½d. As well as the animals all wheeled vehicles attracted a toll.

According to the sign on the cottage wall George Whitbourn was the collector of tolls. The picture must have been taken sometime between April 1871 when George Higlet was still the collector, and 1 November 1877 when the Turnpike Trust was wound up. There were two George Whitbourns in Shalford at that time, father and son, both carpenters. If this is a photograph of George Whitbourn it must be the elder one, born in Shalford in 1804, who lived his whole life in the village. He must have been the last

collector at Shalford Gate and the photograph was perhaps taken to commemorate the end of the era of turnpike roads and toll gates.

The toll-gate was a barrier across the road, opened by the keeper who lived in the adjoining cottage and collected the tolls. During the eighteenth century the major roads in the country were taken over by turnpike trusts, which raised capital for their development and used the tolls to maintain them. In 1758 the road through Shalford village, now the A281, became part of the new Alfold Turnpike. The Austens of Shalford House, like other major landowners, realised the advantages to the district of improved roads and invested money in the turnpike. But local tradition says that they moved the

Early 1900s. Park Cottages are on the left and the toll-gate cottage on the right. A horse and wagon stand by the cottage; the narrow entrance to Pilgrims Way is hard to see.

The same scene in 2007. Park Cottages still stand but the toll-gate cottage on the corner of Pilgrims Way has gone

entrance to their carriage drive to avoid the toll-gate. Maps do appear to bear this out. When the Trust was wound up in 1877 there were four turnpike gates on the road: at Shalford, Bramley, Smithbrook and Alfold. There had also been a gate at Stonebridge in Shalford which was gone by the mid-nineteenth century.

Maintenance of the road was taken over by the Blackheath Highways Board in 1864 and then by Hambledon Rural District Council in 1894. The toll-gate cottage was sold off in 1877, but remained on the corner of Pilgrims Way until 1933. The entrance to Pilgrims Way was much narrower then, and the cottage on the corner created a blind spot for motorists coming from Guildford. The Godwin-Austen estate, busy selling off its fields in building plots, offered a piece of land free of charge for road widening. Despite a request from the Records and Ancient Monuments Committee for the cottage to be saved, and a similar plea from Captain Sant, former Chief Constable of Surrey and champion of Old Shalford, the road widening won the day. The 1934 Ordnance Survey map shows the new layout at the end of Pilgrims Way, the cottage gone, and plots of new houses laid out along Shalford Road. Suburbia was creeping towards the village. Old Shalford was already doomed.

Sources: Photograph of family outside cottage courtesy of Surrey History Centre, ref PH 129/29.
Minutes of Blackheath Highways Board 1868-1881 at Surrey History Centre ref 2196/27/1.
Report of County Council discussion on the fate of the cottage *Surrey Advertiser* 4 February 1933 (at Surrey History Centre).

Searching for The Stranger

The mystery of the Stranger's Grave has exerted a strange fascination. Just who lies beneath this marble simply inscribed 'A Stranger died 2 May 1867 Holy, Holy, Holy, Lord God Almighty, Thy will be done?' It wasn't unusual for unknown people to be buried in the churchyard: occasionally a vagrant was found dead in a ditch or drowned in the river. But these unfortunates were buried at the parish's expense in an unmarked grave. The Stranger's grave belonged to someone of means.

A legend developed that this was someone important (a lady?) who took a house in Shalford and lived here secretly. When she died her identity was made known only to the vicar and churchwardens. I determined to discover the truth, perhaps secretly hoping to find some romantic and tragic story to explain why the Stranger was buried here. But was the reality more prosaic? Who exactly was the Stranger?

The Stranger's grave lies just in front of the Garden of Remembrance in Shalford churchyard

The Shalford burial register has only two adult burials in May 1867: Mary Ann Hatch, aged 55, died on 27 April and buried on 3 May, and Isaac Henry Forster, aged 62, died on 2 May and buried on 6 May. There wasn't another adult burial until September. Mary Ann Hatch wasn't the Stranger: she died on the wrong day and in any case has a grave elsewhere in the churchyard. The West Surrey Family History Society recorded all the gravestone inscriptions in 1976. Isaac Henry Forster does not have a recorded grave. This in itself was not much help: many inscriptions were already illegible by 1976, and some stones had been removed. But his date of death certainly ties up with the Stranger's grave. I must confess to having dismissed him previously, on the strength of the story that the Stranger was a woman. In *More Scenes of Shalford Past* I wrote that the Stranger's burial was not recorded in the parish register. I may now have to eat those words.

The district Deaths Register reveals no other candidate for the Stranger, and Isaac Henry Forster's death was the only one in Shalford registered as 2 May. But registration of deaths was not compulsory until 1876. There was no penalty for failing to register a death, just for refusal to do so if requested by the registrar. If the Stranger was in fact a woman whose identity her relatives were determined to keep secret her burial might still have gone unrecorded in the parish register and the death not notified to the Registrar.

So what else is known about Isaac Henry Forster? The Deaths Register records that he died of cystitis (poor man) and lived at Broadford House. I wouldn't have thought of Broadford as a place where a person could live secretly. It was a busy, bustling little hamlet by the river, with trade and industry centred on Broadford Brewery and Stonebridge Wharf. Broadford House is the large house beside The Parrot, now part of the business park. It belonged to millwright Charles Harris until Frederick Webb, owner of the brewery, bought it in 1866. The rate books reveal that Forster was the tenant from mid-1866. So he *was* a newcomer then, a stranger.

The *Surrey Advertiser* carried a death announcement. Isaac Henry Forster was 'late Registrar and for many years an inhabitant of the Colony of British Guiana.' If he had spent many years abroad before coming to Broadford House he was indeed a stranger. But announcing the death in the newspaper is rather at odds with the Stranger's anonymous grave.

Next stop was the Principal Probate Registry in High Holborn, for a copy of his will. This gave his former address as 'The Rookery', Georgetown, Demerara. I thought of rum and sugar and had a vague idea that Demerara was in the West Indies. It was in fact part of British Guiana, now Guyana, on the South American mainland. Georgetown was – is – the capital. The will gave no other information whatever, apart from the name of his wife, Charlotte Catherine Forster. The nostalgic name of his house, 'The Rookery,' hints at the large British community of merchants, soldiers and civil servants in the colony. Isaac Henry Forster's history reflects the way the world was changing.

Finally the Colonial Office records at The National Archives revealed that he was Registrar for the counties of Demerara and Essequebo, an important and lucrative post. He had taken up his first appointment in the colony in 1822, when he was seventeen years old.

Forty years of the unhealthy West Indies climate took its toll. On doctor's advice he

Broadford House is now part of Broadford Business Park. It has been extended since Isaac Henry Forster lived there. In his time it had a large garden backing onto the river and an open outlook across the Common.

took a year's leave in 1862 for the sake of his health, time which he spent in London. He had been suffering from a chronic infection of the bladder for several years. His return to Demerara in 1863 was short-lived. He gave up his appointment in June 1864 and came back to England, desperate to recover from his illness. Perhaps his final move to Shalford in 1866 was a quest for healthy country air.

Isaac Henry Forster's signature
(The National Archives)

I concluded that he must be the Stranger. Arriving already very ill he would have lived quietly and played no part in village life. He had spent most of his life abroad and may well have felt like a stranger here. His widow left soon after his death and I haven't been able to trace her: perhaps she went abroad again. She probably had immediate practical reasons for placing an announcement of his death in the *Surrey Advertiser*. We will never know if the anonymous inscription on his grave was her choice or his.

I walked down to the churchyard and placed a few late rosebuds on the grave, with a whispered apology in case my curiosity had disturbed his rest. As I stepped back my glance took in three letters on the foot of the grave: 'IHF.' Of course, Isaac Henry Forster. He had been playing a game with me. Lettering that is normally hard to see stood out clearly in the bright autumn sunshine. I had previously read it as 'IHS', the monogram of the name of Jesus often found on gravestones.

So there was never any conspiracy or cover-up. No mysterious lady. I felt a little silly realising that his initials had been on the grave all the time. How easy it is to be swayed by romantic legends. Still, I'm glad I finally learnt the truth: Isaac Henry Forster after a long career in exotic Demerara was buried here, a Stranger on the far side of the ocean.

Sources:
Shalford burial register, Shalford Rate Books, Directories, Monumental Inscriptions recorded by Dr R Mesley and the West Surrey Family History Society, *Surrey Advertiser* on microfilm, all at Surrey History Centre.
Colonial Office records for British Guiana at The National Archives in CO 111,112,115,116.

Many thanks to Stephanie Monk for research at the West Surrey Register Office

Beech House and the Huguenot Connection

Investigating the background of the occupants of yet another grave in the churchyard – William and Ann Lafosse, who lived at Beech House in the early 1800s – I uncovered a tangle of Huguenot families and incidentally discovered the identity of Lieutenant Heneage Girod of the 22nd Regiment of Foot who died in 1838 and whose grave lies beside the path near the Church Room. Not recognising his name as an inhabitant of the village I always wondered if he would have a story to tell. And it's a good one. Like the Lafosses, his village connection is Beech House (the large white house next to the Seahorse).

William Lafosse died in 1805 and his wife Ann in 1811. They came to Shalford in 1798 from Broad Street in the City of London. William may have been a jeweller like his father. He was baptised in 1716 in the French Huguenot church in Threadneedle Street and so attained an impressive 89 years. He was still well-off, the probate valuation of his estate £7,500. The country charms of Shalford have always attracted wealthy people who made their money in the City – nothing changes. I wondered if the Lafosses were related to later tenants of Beech House with a French name – Charles and Mary De St Leu, who moved to Beech House (then called 'Shalford Cottage') in 1828. There didn't seem to be a family connection, but the Lafosses had attended the same London church as Mary De St Leu's parents.

Huguenots were French Protestants who arrived in England during the late seventeenth and early eighteenth centuries in search of freedom to practise their religion. They established their own churches here and the immigrant families intermarried and formed a close social network. Charles De St Leu was an elder of the French Church in Threadneedle Street, and a director of the French Hospital which cared for sick and needy French Protestants in London. His father was a stockbroker; the family lived in Spital Square, an area of London traditionally inhabited by wealthy Huguenot silk weavers and merchants. Highly skilled jewellers and clockmakers were also found among the Huguenots. Charles De St Leu's uncle Daniel De St Leu was watchmaker to the Queen, and examples of his exquisite work can cost around £10,000 when they come up for sale today.

Beech House in The Street

Charles lived in Shalford for sixteen years until his death in 1844. His wife Mary died the following year. They are buried in Kensal Green Cemetery in London. Charles De St Leu left £18,000 when he died, a very large sum, certainly making him the richest man in Shalford outside the landed gentry.

His cousin Heneage Girod was not so fortunate. Charles De St Leu's mother was Anne Girod, from a Huguenot family of Swiss origin, and her brother Abraham, Heneage's father, was a doctor. Heneage Girod must have been visiting at Beech House when he died here on 9 April 1838. In contrast to his cousin his estate was worth only £450. A Lieutenant in the 22nd Foot, he had been eking out life on half pay for 22 years. His death certificate states that he died of 'paralysis' – a stroke, perhaps. But his obituary in the *Gentleman's Magazine* claimed that his death resulted from 'a protracted illness brought on during his services in a tropical climate, and great sufferings when a prisoner in the Isle of France.' Enough to inspire a search for more details of his life.

Born in Liverpool in 1771 he was in partnership as a solicitor in Chichester in the late 1790s. He became a part-time soldier in 1794, just at the start of the French Revolutionary and Napoleonic Wars. Local regiments were raised to defend the country while the regular troops were fighting abroad and Heneage Girod joined firstly the Surrey Fencibles, then the Sussex Militia and the North Hants Militia. After 14 uneventful years on home soil he transferred to a regiment of the line – a decision he had cause to regret. Appointed to the 22nd Foot in May 1809 he sailed for India to join his regiment stationed at Berhampore near Calcutta. But a French squadron was preying on British vessels in the Bay of Bengal and Girod's ship came under attack.

This must have been the action of 18-22 November 1809 when three merchant ships, the *Windham, Charlton* and *United Kingdom*, belonging to the East India Company and carrying 200 troops bound for India, were taken by two French frigates and a corvette. The *Charlton* and *United Kingdom* decided to fight 'for the honor of the Service' although outgunned by the frigates. They surrendered at the end of the first day. The *Windham*, a better sailer and with a more pugnacious captain, mounted a spirited resistance but was forced to surrender to the frigate *La Vénus* after several days' fight and flight. Girod later lamented that if only he had received a wound in the action in which they were taken he would have been entitled to a pension. As a prisoner in one of the frigates he endured 'privations' which, he claimed, 'so radically injured my health as to render me unfit for active service.' If he was aboard *La Vénus* he had to endure a violent storm in which the ship was dismasted and in danger of sinking. The British crew of the *Windham*, prisoners aboard *La Vénus*, managed to save the ship after the French officers had given up and retired to their cabins to wait for the end. By the time the frigate arrived in the Île de France (Mauritius) on 31 December she had run out of fresh water and the only food left was contaminated rice.

The merchant crews were released in gratitude for saving the ship, but the British soldiers were imprisoned on the island to await an exchange between the French and British. In June 1810 the cartel *Harriet* sailed from the Île de France with exchanged prisoners (including the explorer Matthew Flinders). She arrived in Bengal in late July.

It seems likely that Heneage Girod was one of those exchanged, because he was recorded in his regimental muster at Berhampore for the first time in August of that year. Thereafter he was almost permanently absent through illness.

While his regiment joined the campaign to take Mauritius from the French later in 1810 Lt. Girod was left behind sick in Calcutta. He was eventually invalided back to Britain and recovered sufficiently to be given command of the regimental depot on the Isle of Wight. But only a few months later, to his dismay, he was placed on half pay. The peace that followed Waterloo flooded the country with distressed half pay officers, military and naval, for whom the country now had no use and who were forced to live a scrimping life for the rest of their days. On his £82 a year Heneage Girod struggled to afford 'the common necessities of life', let alone the medical care he needed. (For comparison, his cousin paid £60 a year rent for Beech House.) Tropical diseases had exacerbated the effects of hunger, thirst and overcrowded and insanitary conditions in prison. He suffered recurrent malaria and some disease that required three severe surgical operations. Disabled in the service of his country he applied in 1824 to become one of the Poor Knights of Windsor. This would have meant a pension and accommodation in Windsor Castle, but many indigent veterans applied for these coveted posts and Heneage Girod was unsuccessful.

So now he rests in our churchyard. Back full circle – from a churchyard grave to an important village house, Huguenot jewellers and financiers, the British in India and wars with the French, then to the churchyard again and a soldier's grave. The history of the whole world is found in the story of one village and the people who lived here.

Beside the path near the Church Room Heneage Girod lies beneath the flat tombstone.

Sources: Deeds of Beech House ref G111/64 and Shalford Land Tax assessments at Surrey History Centre. Heneage Girod's commissions listed in the London Gazette. His application to become a Poor Knight of Windsor ref HO 44/50 and his record of service WO 12/3883, WO17/124, WO 25/759&1640, in The National Archives. The British Library (India Office records) for reports of the taking of the *Windham, Charlton* and *United Kingdom: IOR/G/2,* 7, 9, 18. TNA Documents Online for Lafosse, De St Leu and Girod wills; De St Leu family tree in *Miscellanea Genealogica et Heraldica* ed W. Bruce Bannerman, 2001; *The Naval History of Great Britain 1793-1820* by William James, London, 1826; The Asiatic Annual Register 1810-1811.
Thanks to Stephanie Monk for details of Heneage Girod's death registration.

Chinthurst

The photograph below is both a record of a vanished way of life and a rare picture of Chinthurst House (more properly known simply as Chinthurst) in Chinthurst Lane, lost to developers in the 1960s.

The picture was taken in 1927 or 1928. The house's new owners, Stanley and Emily Prest, pose by the doorway with two of their grandchildren, John and Joan Prest, who lived nearby at Burnham in Poplar Road. The photo was provided by Mrs Betty Nicholson of Wonersh, another grandchild of Mr and Mrs Prest, who remembers the house well. The downstairs room with the bay window on the right was a large drawing room running the whole depth of the house, with a bedroom above. The corresponding bay-windowed room on the left was a billiard room with Mrs Prest's bedroom and dressing room above. The dormer windows in the roof were staff bedrooms: four staff lived in the house, with a chauffeur/gardener in one staff cottage at the rear (still standing as Little Chinthurst) and the under-gardener in another (now Turrets).

Stanley Prest was a distinguished engineer working with marine steam turbines. Originally from Durham he moved to Shalford from Beckenham. Here he actively participated in village life, holding such positions as vice-chairman of the Cricket Club, vice-chairman of the Men's Club and chairman of the Conservative Association. He was a sidesman at the parish church and a member of the parochial church council. He

Frontage of Chinthurst c 1927, with the owners Stanley and Emily Prest and two of their grandchildren, John and Joan Prest.

died in 1931; his widow Emily remained at Chinthurst until 1944 when she moved next door to Chinthurst Cottage.

Chinthurst stood with its back to Chinthurst Lane and faced west across its gardens and a field that was also part of the property. Beyond a gravel drive and formal flower beds lay a croquet lawn, tennis court, an ornamental pond and a large vegetable garden. There was a path from the bottom of the garden through to Poplar Road – a short cut for family visiting to and from Burnham in the Prests' time.

John Weaver, who owned Summersbury Farm, built Chinthurst around 1834 on part of his farmland. He called the new house Summersbury. Chinthurst Cottage was built some decades earlier, also on land belonging to Summersbury Farm. John Weaver and his wife Mary were living at Chinthurst Cottage on the 1841 census and Mary as a widow was still there ten years later. The large house was let to tenants. Henry Lightfoot, a London solicitor, purchased it in 1868. In 1874 Edwin Ellis the proprietor of Summersbury Tannery bought the remaining land of Summersbury Farm and built himself a large house which he called Summersbury Hall. Henry Lightfoot then changed the name of his own house from Summersbury to Chinthurst.

During the late 1890s Chinthurst and Chinthurst Cottage became part of the new middle-class area of Shalford, where large houses were built on land once part of Poplar Farm and Summersbury Farm. The occupiers of these houses were newcomers to Shalford: civil servants, army officers and retired people living on their own means. The largest of the new houses, situated next to Chinthurst Cottage, was Grantley, or Grantleigh (the original spelling). This house was built on land sold by Edwin Ellis in

View taken in 1927 of the gardens of Chinthurst, facing west across what is now Chinthurst Park.

1893. According to the 1911 census returns Grantley had more rooms (23) than both Summersbury Hall (19) and Chinthurst House (18). It had at least twelve bedrooms and was set in five acres of grounds, with a lodge and coach house. It became a hotel during the Second World War and was sold for development in 1954. Grantley came and went in the space of sixty years although its lodge remains on Chinthurst Lane. Part of Grantley Close extends across the area of the house and its grounds.

Mr. E. H. Everett.

From 1898 Chinthurst was the home of Edwin Hanmer Everett, who served on the parish council and as churchwarden. He died in 1926 leaving a bequest to the parish church for the lovely triptych behind the altar, part of the chancel renovations of 1929. The triptych was painted by Christopher Webb, who is better known for his work in stained glass. The next owners of Chinthurst were the Prests, followed by Mr and Mrs Bailey from 1944-1954. A picture taken during their ownership shows the house covered in Virginia creeper, in contrast to the gleaming white exterior of the 1927 photograph.

Chinthurst shared the fate of many of Shalford's large houses in the mid-twentieth century, sold to a developer and demolished in 1967. Chinthurst Park now stands on the site of the house, its gardens and field beyond. Chinthurst Cottage remains, much altered and extended. It sits with the new estate at its back, facing across the lane towards the green fields at the base of Chinthurst Hill.

Postscript: There is an additional poignancy in the photograph of Chinthurst on page 28. The twelve year-old boy standing next to his grandfather is the John Prest whose name is inscribed on the village war memorial. He joined the Army before the outbreak of the Second World War and achieved the rank of major in the Royal Artillery. After surviving the war he died of peritonitis in Penang (Malaysia) in March 1946 at the age of 31. He is buried in Penang Western Road Cemetery, in one of ten war graves there in the care of the Commonwealth War Graves Commission.

With many thanks to Mrs Betty Nicholson for the 1927 photographs and memories of Chinthurst, and to Mr Phillip Durham of Chinthurst Park.
Thanks to Mrs Maureen Harper for information about Grantley.

Sources
Surrey History Centre: Ref 6677 Nicholson Papers, with notes by Dr Llewellyn, containing deeds of Chinthurst and Chinthurst Cottage. Ref Zg/103 photocopy of Mrs M Bailey's photograph of Chinthurst c 1954.
Photograph of Edwin Hanmer Everett from *Surrey at the Opening of the Twentieth Century,* by W.E. Hitchin, 1907.

Edwin Ellis and Summersbury

During the last two decades of the nineteenth century Edwin Ellis was probably the most influential man in Shalford. The builder of Summersbury Hall and the owner of Summersbury Tannery, he was also a widely respected agriculturalist. As a wealthy industrialist, farmer and landowner he played a significant role in local politics. He was the first chairman of Shalford Parish Council, represented the district on Surrey County Council, was Chairman of the Highways and Bridges Committee, JP for Surrey, Governor of Wye Agricultural College, Governor of the County Hospital, President of the Shalford Institute and Chairman of Managers of Shalford School for twenty years.

Edwin Ellis inherited Summersbury Tannery from his father James Ellis, and for over forty years was head of the firm of Edwin Ellis and Company, in Bermondsey and Shalford. The firm was well-known for the production of sole leather, or 'Ellis Crops.' The British Army marched on Shalford leather. During the First World War it took the firm's whole output and the skilled tannery workers were exempted from military service.

Edwin Ellis (1833-1913)

Edwin Ellis bought Summersbury Farm in 1874. He was already the occupier of a considerable stretch of neighbouring agricultural land. Like his father before him he was the tenant of Chinthurst Farm, carrying on a market gardening business there in partnership with one of his sons. (He also grew fruit at Nurscombe Farm in Bramley.) His farmland extended to over 400 acres – of which 350 acres was pasture for 300 sheep and 100 cattle. He was a well-known breeder of Southdown sheep and won prizes worth thousands of pounds in this country, on the Continent, in the colonies and in America. At the 1889 International Exhibition in Paris he took nearly all the awards for Southdowns. On the dispersal of the flock in 1906 purchasers included Edward VII, the Duke of Northumberland and the Duke of Devonshire. Some of Edwin Ellis's Shalford sheep travelled to New Zealand.

Edwin was born at Artington Manor Farm into a well-established but not particularly wealthy farming family. Instead of going to public school he was educated privately by a tutor. The family were staunch Unitarians and Edwin Ellis became senior trustee of the Unitarian church in Guildford. In the 1870s he was a strong supporter of the Liberation Society, a movement by nonconformists which aimed to disestablish and disendow the Church of England. Ellis believed that the religious and educational life of the country would flourish as a result. In politics he was a staunch Liberal. Edwin Ellis's educational, religious and political background was therefore different from that

The former Village Hall in Station Road, otherwise known as the Queens Hall, built by Edwin Ellis for the Shalford Institute in 1886, and designed by Henry Peak

Edwin Ellis's initials above the door of the Queens Hall

of most other wealthy influential men in the district. But his impartiality, sound good sense and great ability made him respected everywhere. When he died the deeply Tory *Surrey Advertiser* (which thirty-five years earlier had condemned his Unitarian and political beliefs) claimed that 'there was no man whose opinion on matters of local government carried more weight.'

He was very much a self-made man, conscious of the limitations of his education and when young took evening classes and elocution lessons to improve himself. It was this background that led him to champion the Shalford Institute, with its programme of educational and recreational activities: lectures, concerts and entertainments. The Institute used to meet in the village school, but when Station Road was developed in 1886 Edwin Ellis decided to build a Village Hall there as a home for the Institute. The new Hall was designed by Guildford architect Henry Peak and contained a large room for lectures and assemblies, a reading room and a refreshment room. The building cost Edwin Ellis £1945. When he died in 1913 his will provided for the sale of the Hall to a trust for £2,000, so that it could be kept for the benefit of the village. But the Hall's Management Committee could not raise the funds, and during the First World War the Institute struggled, with many members away. Eventually the Institute lost the Hall, which in 1931 was taken over by the British Legion.

The purchase of Summersbury Farm enabled Edwin Ellis to build a handsome new house, Summersbury Hall, a property appropriate to his wealth and status. At his death in 1913 his estate was valued at £46,000 – about £2.5 million today. However, anyone wanting a mansion like Summersbury Hall now, with its gardens and parkland, would need to be worth a lot more than that. Summersbury Hall became the fourth great house of Shalford, smaller than, but in the same bracket as the Godwin-Austens' Shalford House, Francis Eastwood's Gosden House, and John Renton's Bradstone Brook. The wealthy men of the district considered it their duty to serve the community and assumed the paternalist role towards the poorer classes that had traditionally belonged to the landed gentry. The grounds of Shalford House and Bradstone Brook hosted summer treats for the schoolchildren. At Summersbury Hall Mr and Mrs Ellis entertained the aged poor of the parish to a roast dinner each New Year. Entertainments followed the food – a magic lantern show and a performance by hand-bell ringers from Bramley featured in 1881. Afterwards the old men were plied with tobacco and warm grog, while in another room the women received tea 'and other comforts' *(Surrey Advertiser* 15 January 1881*).*

Summersbury Hall was purchased by William Sydney Dixon in 1923. He also owned substantial property in Scotland. He himself was a Scot, educated at Glenalmond and Oxford, and although called to the bar in 1908 did not practice. He devoted his energy to public service: as a member of Shalford parish council, a manager of Shalford School, as churchwarden, and as Treasurer then Chairman of the Guildford Diocesan Board of Finance. His only son, Andrew Dixon, a former Captain in the Manchester Regiment, died of cancer in 1943; his name is on the village war memorial. William Dixon moved out of Summersbury during the Second World War, when the house was used as a Babies' Hostel and Nursery Training School. After the war the house was requisitioned by the Government and divided into flats which for twelve years were occupied as part of a programme of 'housing the inadequately housed'. The grounds of the house and its surrounding farmland were covered with new roads during the 1950s. The house itself was sold off as flats in 1966.

Summersbury Hall, designed for Edwin Ellis by Guildford architect Henry Peak in 1874.

Sources
Surrey Advertiser: report of Liberation Meeting, 25 November 1878; Edwin Ellis's obituary 9 August 1913; Mr. Dixon's obituary 30 July 1966. Surrey History Centre: Surrey County Council file of buildings requisitioned by the Government Ac 1346/43

Trellis Cottage

L iterally pretty as a picture, Trellis Cottage has featured on Christmas cards and calendars and its distinctive beehive box hedge once appeared in an American book on topiary. Previous names of the house - Tickners, Heathfield, Copper's Cottage - hint at something of its 400-year history.

The cottage lies on the corner of Horsham Road and Poplar Road, facing the Common. For the first two centuries of its existence it was surrounded by fields on the other three sides. The timber-framed building dates from just before or just after 1600. In recent years it has been extended on both sides without losing character, although the stepped

Trellis Cottage in 2007

chimney is no longer visible. The frontage has been completely rebuilt in brick, but the back still reveals the precise square panels of the timber framing. The house escaped the cottage orné treatment – wavy-edged bargeboards, crested ridge tiles and gables over the upper windows - meted out to some of the other houses belonging to the Godwin-Austen estate in the 1850s; despite the extensions its appearance is therefore perhaps more authentic than most.

Internally it retains many original features such as carpenters' assembly marks cut sharply on the timbers in Roman numerals, a large inglenook, and a burn on the hearth beam from a taper rush light. Another practical, if macabre, relic of former times is the 'coffin hole': a beam which slides through the wall to allow a corpse to be lowered downstairs without the indignity of negotiating the narrow staircase. The hole could also be used to hoist furniture to the upper floor. The cottage kept its earth floors

Trellis Cottage in 1837

well into the twentieth century. At one time a policeman lodged there, giving rise to its unofficial name of 'Copper's Cottage.' In 1948 the owner Florence Goodchild sold it to Ambrose Forsythe, a gardening journalist. He was responsible for creating the distinctive miniature beehive box hedge. The trellis that gave the cottage its name covered the front of the house in the early 1900s.

Two William Tickners, father and son, successively owned the house with its garden, orchard and two fields behind (about five acres of land) in the late eighteenth century. The house was called Heathfield and occupied by a George Edwards in 1792, when William Tickner of Wonersh sold it to Robert Austen of Shalford House. The fields were added to adjoining land owned by the Austen estate and became part of Poplar Farm. The cottage was let to agricultural workers. Edwin Ellis of Summersbury Hall bought Poplar Farm in 1886 from the Godwin-Austen estate, paying £3,000 for 31 acres of arable and pasture, the farmhouse itself and two cottages – one of which was Trellis Cottage.

Poplar Farm, then known as Chinthurst Lane Farm, in 1837. The house still stands as Poplars in Chinthurst Lane.

The character of the area changed rapidly during the 1890s. Land was becoming more profitable for building than agriculture and Edwin Ellis intended Poplar Farm for development, selling off some plots and building large houses to let on others. Mrs Ann Garraway bought Trellis Cottage and an adjacent plot of land in 1891 and built Tyn-y-Llwyn (later called Conford House). On the other side of Trellis Cottage Poplar Road was constructed, with large new houses - Oaklands and Burnham - and similar houses appeared on the Bramley road: Holbrook, Denbigh House, Commonside and The Marlows. The trend continued during the twentieth century, leaving all the farmland of Poplar Farm and Summersbury Farm covered by housing. In recent years the Victorian and Edwardian houses have either been converted to flats or demolished and replaced by new development, leaving Trellis Cottage sandwiched between much later buildings as a solitary reminder of old Shalford.

Sources

Documents relating to the purchase of Trellis Cottage by Robert Austen at Surrey History Centre ref G43/179; Report of the Domestic Buildings Research Group and other historic material courtesy of Ian and Wendy Camfield, current owners of Trellis Cottage.
1837 drawings of Trellis Cottage and Poplar Farm ref G111/9/29/62 & 27 courtesy of Surrey History Centre and Lt Col R H Godwin-Austen DL.

Building Shalford
(and a story about Lutyens' trousers)

The fun with local history is the unexpected gems that come to light. In this case a connection between a firm of Shalford builders and someone as famous as Sir Edwin Lutyens. The name Mitchell is always cropping up in records of Victorian Shalford: in newspaper reports, in minutes of Vestry and parish council meetings, in the parish registers and rate books. The Mitchells were builders and brickmakers. Evidence of them is all around: the Old Vicarage on Shalford Road, Mitchells Row by the Common, Shalford Cemetery Chapel, St Michael's Church Peasmarsh, St Thomas's Church Chilworth, houses in Chilworth New Road, the British Legion/Queen's Hall and neighbouring houses in Station Road are all their work. In fact Station Road itself was a Mitchell development.

The first of the family to arrive in Shalford seems to have been builder Nimrod Mitchell, who was born in Wisborough Green in Sussex in 1793, but married at Bramley in 1817. Mid-century census returns show him living at Gosden Common, next to houses called The Barracks. These were supposedly built with reused bricks from the Militia Barracks in Guildford. The barracks were demolished in 1818 so just possibly Nimrod Mitchell had something to do with building the houses at Gosden Common. However, it was Nimrod's son Edward who started to make it in a big way. He moved to Orchard House in Shalford village – a house owned by the Austen estate and already in use as a builders' yard. He employed 3 men there in 1851, but by 1871 his workforce had increased to 38. At that time, as well as the Shalford premises, he had a house and yard in Hare Lane Farncombe.

In 1857 he rebuilt Shalford's Vicarage, and enlarged it in 1865. The plans he drew up are in the London Metropolitan Archive. The house was an imposing statement of the authority of the church in mid-Victorian England – eight bedrooms, drawing room, dining room and library, as well as kitchen, pantry, scullery, and store rooms. At the other end of the social scale Edward Mitchell was responsible for building Mitchells Row, ten four-roomed labourer's cottages on a slip of land near the Common. They may be charming now, but they acquired an insanitary reputation not long after they were built, and were occupied by some of Shalford's poorest families.

The second Edward Mitchell (1845-1914)

After his death Edward Mitchell's sons Edward and William became Mitchell Brothers of Shalford and Godalming. The late nineteenth century was a boom time for builders. In 1886 the second Edward Mitchell paid £1200 for two pieces of land between the railway and Kings Road; some of this land was in use as allotments, but with a growing population and thriving local industries there was a desperate need for more housing. In his new Station Road Edward Mitchell built the Village Hall (later the Queen's Hall and British Legion), a gift to the village from tanner Edwin Ellis and designed by Guildford architect Henry Peak. He also built himself a large new house in Station Road – Pathfield House – and moved his yard there. Berks Pharmaceuticals took over the site in the 1960s. More recently the area has been redeveloped: one of the new roads is called Mitchells Close.

As one of the largest employers in the village Edward Mitchell had a high profile and made a strong contribution to public life. He was a trustee of the village school; he regularly attended meetings of the Vestry, which acted as the civil parish's governing body, and served for several years as a member of Shalford's Burial Board. He was vicar's churchwarden for 21 years and sidesman for 15 years. Ratepayers elected him to serve on the new parish council in 1894. By the 1890s Mitchell Brothers' annual works outing was one of the highlights of Shalford's calendar: a trip to Ramsgate and Margate one year saw 200 people – Mitchell employees, their families, and other parishioners – embark on a special train from Shalford at 6.35 am. The vicar, Hugh Huleatt, already on holiday at Herne Bay, chartered a steamboat and treated 154 of the party to a sea trip which 'the majority enjoyed immensely' (the rest were presumably seasick). The author of the report in the *Surrey Advertiser* suggested that this was 'the largest party of Shalfordians at sea in the memory of the oldest inhabitant.' It must have been a very tired party that arrived back in Shalford at 11pm, when 'hearty cheers were accorded Mr Mitchell.'

Sunnyside (now The Badgers Holt), on the corner of Station Road in the early 1900s.

37

According to the 1891 Poor Rate assessments various members of the Mitchell family owned around 30 houses beside the Common and in Station Road. One of these was the first house on the right in Station Road. Maybe Edward Mitchell always intended it for his son Nimrod – the fourth generation of Mitchell builders in Shalford. Newly-married Nimrod Mitchell and his wife Louisa moved into the house, which they called Sunnyside, in 1899.

And the Lutyens story at last. Edwin Lutyens' first large commission as a very young man was Crooksbury House in Farnham, built for Arthur Chapman in 1890 by Mitchell Brothers of Shalford. Later in life Lutyens confessed to having being so nervous that he only visited the site once the workmen had gone home for the day. Not every day however, for Mitchell tradition has it that Lutyens once sat down on a newly-painted garden seat whilst discussing the plans, and had to go home in Nimrod's trousers. It's the little human touch that brings it all to life. Lutyens was only 21 in 1890, two

Lutyens' sketch of the garden terrace wall at Crooksbury House. An arrow points to a seat. Was this the seat that ruined his trousers? (RIBA archive)

years older than Nimrod, and they must have been about the same size. The RIBA archive at the V&A contains letters from Lutyens to Mrs Chapman which mention 'Mitchell the builder' – with a sketch of the garden terrace wall showing a built-in seat. Was this the very seat that ruined Lutyens' trousers? Crooksbury also saw the start of the collaboration between Lutyens and Gertrude Jekyll. A descendant of the Mitchells has a sideboard said to have been carved by one of the workmen who was incapacitated through injury – the sideboard made to Jekyll's design and under her instruction.

Edward Mitchell died in 1914 at Sunnyside, aged 69. Nimrod carried on the business but the war caused difficulties, with private building forbidden; in any case labour was scarce with most able-bodied men in the forces. Nimrod left Shalford in 1920 and moved to Balham. After building Shalford for a century, the Mitchells' link with the village was broken.

Sources
Surrey History Centre: *Surrey Advertiser*; Shalford Poor Rate books ref LA6/23; Shalford Vestry Minutes PSH/SHD/21/1. London Metropolitan Archive: plans of Shalford Vicarage 1857 and 1865 ref DWOP S.52 and 53.
Lutyens' letters relating to Crooksbury House in the RIBA archive at the V&A ref LU E/33/10 (1-13). Many thanks to John Mitchell for family information and photographs, and to Judy Moss for inspiring the research.

'A Fearful Railway Accident'
Peasmarsh Tuesday 9 September 1873

❝ What is the matter with that train?' exclaimed a man on the road at Artington, seeing carriages rise into the air. He was waiting for Benjamin Palmer, a young Godalming butcher who had stopped to help a drover whose bullocks had strayed through an open gate into a lane leading to the railway line.

Palmer turned back six of the seven bullocks towards the main road, but the seventh continued down the lane, leapt the gate at the end 'like a dog' and set off up the track at the very moment the Guildford-bound train steamed into view. The driver braked, whistled and threw the engine into reverse but had no chance of stopping in time. The blow from the engine tossed the animal forward between the rails – the engine passed over it but the front carriage was derailed, seven others piling with it down the embankment.

On that hot Tuesday afternoon about 70 passengers lay tumbled in the wreckage, with three dead and 30 injured. Many had joined the train at Milford and Godalming. At Milford Georgiana Martin, just twenty-two and the station master's daughter, boarded the train together with the vicar of Milford, the Rev Henry Salmon, and two of his sons. Among 15 or so getting on at Godalming was Edwin Crouch of Shalford, rate collector of the parish and a journalist for the *Surrey Advertiser*. With him was 'Mr Mitchell junior of Farncombe' – one of the sons of builder Edward Mitchell who had premises in Shalford and Farncombe. Also from Godalming were John Debenham junior, a solicitor's managing clerk; 10 year-old Frederick Lyon on his way to boarding school for the autumn term; and Rhoda Bridger, wife of grocer Henry Bridger in Hart Lane, with her nine-month old baby Richard. Guildford passengers included articled clerk Gerald Smallpeice and Maria McCarthy, a fish-hawker from Quarry Street. From further afield came Frances Chapman, on her way from Shanklin to be a bridesmaid in Guildford, young Emily Vivash, a servant in Bayswater, and housekeeper Emily Dilloway from Midhurst. Also passengers were two members of brewery families whose firms were becoming household names. Alfred Courage was travelling with his young family and two servants, both of whom were injured. Sixty-one year-old Fanny Evans, a clergyman's widow, was a Charrington by birth. Her badly broken arm was amputated at the Royal Surrey County Hospital.

Nineteen-year-old Emma Clayden was the daughter of a political journalist and author living in London's Tavistock Square. She was travelling with her sister, two brothers, one of whom was a child, and his nurse. Later that same day she sent a graphic account of events to the *Surrey Advertiser*. Moments before the accident she saw Palmer 'waving his stick and looking terribly frightened.' Then the whistle, an awful jolt, the family thrown forward in a heap, more jolts, a smashing and crashing, clouds of dust, a shower of glass and splinters, then silence broken by the nurse's exclamation asking for the child. None of them was hurt - saved, Emma believed, by the seat cushions that fell on top of them. The buffers and corner of the next carriage had broken completely through into their compartment.

Rescuers quickly appeared, walking along the tops of the carriages to reach the occupants. Railway workers on an embankment nearby brought tools to break the carriages open. Others hurried to the spot. Edwin Crouch noticed a Shalford neighbour, carpenter George Whitbourn, among the rescuers. Passengers able to extricate themselves joined in the rescue, including John Debenham, slightly hurt himself, and the Rev. Salmon, whose younger son was badly bruised. Emma Clayden's little brother, terrified of being buried alive, was hauled to safety and sat beside the railway crying. His elder brother wanted to be helping and climbed out. Emma waited for a ladder to arrive. Then: 'What a sight! Nearly the whole train lying on its side along the embankment. Some of the carriages and many of the people were almost buried in the earth. All around lay wounded and suffering people, many of whom appeared to be children.' There was a lot of blood: many had been cut by broken glass and splinters. The worst cases were laid in a meadow by the line and given brandy by Miss Ellis from Artington Manor Farm. Seven or more doctors summoned from Guildford and a police surgeon among the passengers tended to the wounded. The Guildford hotels sent their carriages to take the injured to hospital.

The seond railway carriage was buried in sand which half-filled it, with only the limbs of the occupants visible. Two women were pronounced dead almost immediately, suffocated in the sand. Rescuers dug frantically for the baby whom they could hear choking, but couldn't reach him in time. Emily Vivash was saved by men scooping the

Photograph taken by Mr. Crane of the Surrey Photographic Company
(courtesy of Guildford Museum)

sand from her face and giving her water until she could be freed, with her arm badly broken. Edwin Crouch saw the bodies brought out: first a well-dressed young lady – Georgiana Martin – then a woman with an infant - Rhoda Bridger and her baby.

Four of the injured remained in hospital the following weekend: Fanny Evans recovering from her amputation, Emily Vivash and the Rev. Frederick Pelham Griffith from Sutton each with a broken arm, and Emily Dilloway with contusion. They even had a royal visitor. Prince Arthur, Queen Victoria's third son, an army officer stationed at Aldershot, rode over to the hospital to enquire after the patients, and visited the scene of the accident where the carriages remained. All week crowds flocked to view the wreckage, their excitement fanned by rumours that a woman's body still lay under the debris. At Artington Manor Farm sightseers broke down Mr Ellis's hedges and the police had to restrain people from venturing onto the railway line. The carriages were removed on the Sunday following the accident, the sensation-seekers disappointed when no body was discovered.

Georgiana Martin's funeral took place at Milford, conducted by the vicar Henry Salmon who had survived the accident. Rhoda and Richard Bridger were buried at Nightingale Road Cemetery in Godalming. Both funerals drew large crowds. Two years later Henry Bridger, grocer and Godalming town councillor, married a recently-widowed neighbour, Anne Covey. Of the injured, the Rev. Griffith went off to Guatemala to become a university professor and sub-director of the Colegio Militar. Fanny Evans died of cancer three years later. Of those who left an account of their experience, Edwin Crouch continued to write reports of local events for the *Surrey Advertiser*; he became clerk to every committee in Shalford and in the 1890s was village postmaster. The strong-minded Emma Clayden married a doctor, had four daughters and a son and lived in Battersea.

The scene of the accident today, between Peasmarsh footbridge and Shalford Junction

41

Accidents on Victorian railways were much more common than today. The Rail Accident Reports for 1873 reveal 58 accidents or incidents resulting in death or injury on the London and South Western Railway alone. Six passengers were killed that year, three through their own carelessness. But 27 railway employees died in the same period, largely through a cavalier attitude towards their own safely.

Some good came out of the Peasmarsh accident because it drew attention to the injury and damage caused by the lack of continuous brakes, which resulted in carriages smashing into and riding over one another. The jury returned a verdict of 'Accidental Death' with a recommendation that continuous brakes be fitted to trains in future.

For the helpful young butcher, Benjamin Palmer, it was his second nightmare experience with the railway. He was walking beside the line a few years earlier when his basket of meat was clipped by a train; he was 'whirled like a ball' into a field and came to thirty yards away with his dog licking his face. Apprehensive of trains ever since he bravely assisted in the rescue but suffered from nervous strain afterwards.

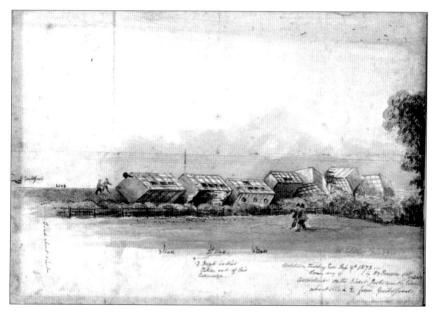

Drawing of the scene by Guildford artist Henry Prosser made the same evening from 'Mr Ellis's meadow.' He notes that the embankment was eight feet high, and that the second carriage from the left is where the fatalities occurred.
(courtesy of Guildford Museum)

Main Sources: *Surrey Advertiser* 13 & 20 September 1873; Supplement to *The Illustrated London News* 20 September 1873; RAIL 1053/184 at The National Archives.

St Michael's Peasmarsh

Hidden away in the trees by Unstead Wood St Michael's reached its 120th anniversary in 2008. A pretty little building of the Arts and Crafts era it originated as a Mission Room intended to serve the Peasmarsh end of Shalford parish.

In December 1887 Francis Eastwood of Gosden House sold the land for £20, subject to certain trusts, to the Vicar of Shalford and the trustees of Peasmarsh Church - the Vicar and Mr Eastwood, Miss Emilia Margaret Guthrie from Tilthams (a few years later Lutyens built a large house for her on Chinthurst Hill) and Mr George Webb, owner of Broadford Brewery. The architect was William Lower of Guildford; the building was constructed by Mitchell Brothers of Shalford. The construction costs and fees, amounting to £405, were raised by subscriptions.

A congregation of 170 crammed into the room for the service to mark its opening on 4 July 1888. The service was conducted by the Vicar, Hugh Huleatt and his son the Reverend Charles Huleatt who, according to the *Surrey Advertiser*, gave a 'very forcible and eloquent address'. Charles Huleatt was a popular figure in the parish; he had acted as his father's curate and played cricket on the village green. He perished with his wife and children in the Messina earthquake of 1908 – a commemorative tablet to the family is in the south aisle of the parish church.

The Mission Room, alternatively called the Peasmarsh Church Room, was intended for 'all useful purposes in connection with and for the benefit of the parish': these included services taken by a lay reader, and a Sunday School. The room soon housed a flourishing night school on three evenings a week and Miss Guthrie promised a library. At first services at the new Church Room were erratic. Charles Barrington Walters, Shalford's vicar from 1897, is credited with initiating regular Sunday services in the afternoon, with a monthly Holy Communion at 8 am. It was only in the 1960s during the Reverend Horth's time as vicar that moves were made to give the Peasmarsh Church Room a proper dedication, and in discussions in 1966 St Michael emerged as favourite. The new vicar, the Reverend Ken Morgan, conducted the dedication ceremony on St Michael's Day, 29 September 1966.

The Peasmarsh Church Room soon gained a sister Mission Room at

St Michael's, Peasmarsh

Chilworth, or Shalford Hamlet, at the opposite end of the parish. The Hamlet Church Room was built in 1895, also constructed by Mitchell Brothers, and designed by architect William Howard Seth-Smith, who also designed Wonersh United Reformed Church. The Hamlet Room is now St Thomas's Church and regarded as something of an architectural gem. It was built not as a church but as an educational and recreational institute for his workers by George Unwin, proprietor of the Chilworth printing works. It cost him £1200, but when the works relocated to Woking after a fire in December 1895 he sold the institute to the vicar and churchwardens of Shalford for only £850. He also contributed £100 to the purchase fund.

St Thomas's, Chilworth

The Hamlet building was larger and better equipped than that at Peasmarsh. Besides the room adapted for the church, capable of holding 250 people, it had a second room and a caretaker's room. The Bishop of Southampton performed the opening service in June 1896. The Bishop of Guildford dedicated the building to St Thomas in 1919. It seems that St Thomas's always enjoyed a higher profile than St Michael's. With the increase in population at Chilworth St Thomas's finally split from Shalford in 1937 to form a separate parish.

Postscript: The architect of St Michael's, William Lower, sat on the inquest jury following the railway accident at Peasmarsh in 1873 (see previous chapter). Two years earlier he had had his own dramatic moment and was hailed as a hero for rescuing two young men from drowning near St Catherine's Lock early one August morning. The *Surrey Advertiser* recorded his 'Noble Conduct' and that he was a good diver and excellent swimmer. Before public baths were built in Guildford the area below the lock was the only place where men and boys could bathe, only permitted early in the morning and after 9 pm. Previously the sight of naked men and boys running around on the towpath had scandalised railway passengers and ladies out for a walk. Ladies of course couldn't bathe at all.

Sources
Report of opening of Peasmarsh Church Room in the *Surrey Advertiser* 7 July 1888; opening of the Hamlet Church Room *Surrey Advertiser* 6 June 1896; William Lower's 'Noble Conduct' reported in the *Surrey Advertiser* 12 August 1871 (all on microfilm at Surrey History Centre).

Thanks to Sheila Mitchell for information about St Michaels's

A Christmas Card from 1907

Just over a century ago this charming sketch was sent as a Christmas card to Rosina Elliott in Station Road.

Rosina Elliott kept a draper's shop at no 6 Station Road - 'R. Elliott Draper & Stationer' - and the card seems to be a self-portrait of one of Rosina's friends or relatives just entering the shop. Clothes are hanging in the window; just to the lady's left as she enters is a display of 'Toilet Combs' and what looks like a little teddy fastened to the wall.

Rosina Elliott took over the shop with a partner, a Miss Jenner, around 1903. For the previous sixteen years or so it had been a butcher's shop, built at the same time as the Shalford Institute (later the British Legion) adjoining. Both belonged to Edwin Ellis of Summersbury Hall and were built in 1886 when Station Road was developed by prominent Shalford builder Edward Mitchell. Surrey Directories show that the shop was still known as Elliotts following Rosina's marriage to Oliver Crompton in 1908. A business card printed after 1910 advertises it as 'R. Elliott, Milliner, Dressmaker and Fancy Draper.' Directory entries changed to 'Oliver R Crompton, draper' in 1920. Around this time the Cromptons and the drapery business moved next door to 4 Station Road, and no 6 became a sweet shop run by Miss Annie Cornes.

I bought the card on eBay with a whole bundle of family photographs, including the one on the next page of Rosina's husband Oliver Crompton and their baby outside the shop at no 6. The same kind of clothes as in the drawing can be seen hanging in the window. Pictures of Oliver as a young man show a good-humoured, keenly intelligent face with an impressive handlebar moustache and a head of unruly, wiry dark hair. The only photos of Rosina, or Rose, as she was known to friends and family, are those taken with her husband and

Oliver Crompton holding the baby outside the draper's shop at 6 Station Road sometime between 1910 and 1913

children: an attractive, serious woman, hair drawn back in a bun. Their son Samuel rides a donkey on the beach, then, older, he stands to attention in his sailor-suit, hand raised in salute. But behind these images of comfortable family life lies sadness. There was another baby. Rosina and Oliver married rather late in life (for the time) when she was 39 and he was 45. Samuel arrived a year later, in 1909, and in 1912 Edna Ruth was born. She died aged 16 months in January 1914. So which baby is Oliver holding? Is it Samuel or Edna?

The Cromptons continued next door at no 4 throughout World War II. Rosina died in 1940 at the age of 72. Oliver survived her by 15 years and died in 1955 aged 92. By then he was living in Dapdune Road, Guildford. Samuel became a building surveyor and died in 2004 at the age of 95. Perhaps that's how the photographs ended up on eBay. Sad.

No 6 remained a sweet shop and grocers. Bryants grocers and confectioners took over in the 1940s. For a few years in the 1990s it was a saddlers – Stirrups - with a life-size plastic horse called Kevin standing outside. Now, a sign of the times, the shop has been incorporated into the house, the shop window has gone and a porch has been added to the front of the house. Another instalment in the restless rearrangements of Station Road.

Sources: Shalford rate books, Kelly's Directories, at Surrey History Centre. Probate Records at the Principal Probate Registry, High Holborn; photographs bought on eBay.

On a Hillside at Guildford: a Domestic Ideal.

The neighbours weren't keen on it, apparently. Too much glass, too square and upright, too foreign-looking somehow. It didn't blend in with its surroundings nor pay homage to the idea of an Englishman's ideal residence, as expressed in the best Arts and Crafts tradition.

Artist and critic Roger Fry designed his own house, Durbins, in Chantry View Road in 1909, one of the first houses to be constructed in the newly-laid out Warwicks Bench area. The Surrey volume of Pevsner's *Buildings of England* describes its location as 'an odd area…laid out with expensive houses around 1900 and still [with] open country beyond.' Quite where the oddness lies isn't clear: perhaps in the suburban assortment of large houses in large plots overlooking what is still a very picturesque landscape of wooded hills and river meadows. Whatever he meant, Pevsner was very impressed with the innovative design of Durbins, and contrasted it favourably with three Baillie-Scott houses nearby, which he condemned as 'fundamentally timid.'

The Arts and Crafts style had grown out of a nostalgic, idealised view of a pre-industrial England of snug cottages, comfortable farmhouses and ancient manor houses, built of local materials by local craftsmen. In late Victorian and Edwardian England only the rich could afford the 'traditional' houses and gardens designed by Lutyens, Jekyll, Voysey, Baillie-Scott and others whose work found a ready home in a Surrey landscape already attracting London lawyers and money men. Their ideal home featured gables and timbering, even turrets, leaded windows and panelled walls. By

1909 a watered-down version of Arts and Crafts had become the English suburban style. No wonder Roger Fry's house came as a bit of a shock.

His inspiration came more from the continent than rural England: he created an Italianate townhouse in the countryside. Fry rather relished his neighbours' disapproval. In contrast to their deliberately picturesque houses he adopted a severe, almost classical style. He preferred symmetry, light and high ceilings to the cottagey mainstream designs. Durbins' most radical feature was a galleried central room he called the 'house place', two storeys high, two columns of windows flooding the house with light. Roger Fry was responsible for introducing cubism and post-impressionist art into Britain. His two Post-Impressionist Exhibitions in London in 1910 and 1912 – planned at Durbins and featuring works by Gaugin, Cézanne, Matisse and Van Gogh - attracted an uncomprehending critical onslaught in the same way that his own house was rejected by his conservative neighbours.

True, the house was not very 'Guildford'. But what made Durbins special was not simply architectural inspiration. Fry's wife had become ill shortly after their marriage and they moved from London to the country on the advice of her doctor. Fry's dream was to create a family home, a true domestic ideal, reflecting the way his family lived rather than primarily displaying money and status. Fry came from a well-known and wealthy Quaker family (an uncle founded the firm of Fry chocolate manufacturers) but was not rich himself. The price of the property was a stretch - £600 for the acre of land and £1,000 to build the house. He designed his house with central heating and a dumb waiter because he couldn't afford the servants taken for granted by his wealthier neighbours. The interior was pared down to the point of austerity, with bare plastered walls and creosoted woodwork.

The house was placed at the rear of the plot to take advantage of the stunning views. Fry ingeniously built the house into the hill so that its rear aspect is lower and cosier than the imposing frontage. The garden was as important as the house. From the gallery of the 'house place' the garden appears as both as an extension of the house and acts as foreground to the dramatic landscape beyond. With Gertrude Jekyll Fry laid out a symmetrical series of terraces, much more formal than her usual designs. Jekyll supplied 600

The entrance at the rear of the house

plants from her own grounds at Munstead. Fry commissioned sculptures from Eric Gill for both house and garden. Unsurprisingly, given Gill's proclivities, Fry had to reject one of the statues as likely to embarrass visiting ladies involved in his sister's charitable work. Gill replaced it with one slightly less erotic, *The Virgin*, which Fry positioned in front of Matisse's *La Danse* in his second Post-Impressionist Exhibition.

Fry's close friends in the Bloomsbury circle of artists and writers admired Durbins. Virginia Woolf, Fry's biographer, loved the house. Her sister Vanessa Bell painted with Duncan Grant two life-size nudes in the style of Matisse for the entrance hall; Fry added a third naked figure, said to resemble Bell. All very bohemian - the neighbours' reactions to the mural are not recorded. Bell and Grant started a mosaic of tennis players, never finished, in the summerhouse. They and Fry sketched the panoramic vistas across the river valley, as yet uninterrupted by houses. So the views from Chantry View Road became part of early twentieth century British art, and at least one crossed the Atlantic. Fry's *The Artist's Garden at Durbins* is held in the Paul Mellon collection at the Yale Centre for British Art.

Roger Fry was described by Sir Kenneth Clarke as 'incomparably the greatest influence on taste since Ruskin...Insofar as taste can be changed by one man it was changed by Roger Fry.' This must make him one of the most important people to have graced the local scene, albeit fleetingly. For sadly Fry's dream did not last. His wife's mental health broke down completely and she was confined to an institution almost as soon as Durbins was built. The outbreak of war in 1914 put a severe strain on Fry's finances and by the end of the war he had to move. He let the house to the Strachey family. Lytton Strachey finished writing his *Eminent Victorians* there.

Today, Durbins has lost its power to shock. It is not so visible now, having given up part of its garden to a new bungalow, and blends into the eclectic mix of styles produced by later building phases in the road. Over the years a procession of artists, writers and critics have visited and admired the house. Despite being well-known to Bloomsbury fans and lovingly tended by its owners it has attracted little local interest. Now, as it reaches its centenary, Durbins deserves more recognition.

With thanks to Mr and Mrs J H Lukas of Durbins

Sources
The Buildings of England – Surrey, Ian Nairn and Nikolaus Pevsner, 1962; *Roger Fry – Art and Life*, Frances Spalding, 1980; *Roger Fry*, Virginia Woolf, 1940; *Roger Fry, anecdotes*, Clive Bell, published by Cecil Woolf 1997; *Roger Fry's Durbins: A House and its Meanings*, Christopher Reed, published by Cecil Woolf 1999.

Captain Hastings and Captain Sant

Captain Henry Cadogan Hastings, 1813-1906

Captain Hastings and Captain Sant were the first two Chief Constables of Surrey. They served nearly 80 years between them, from 1851 to 1930, and both lived in Shalford, albeit briefly in the case of Captain Hastings. He is listed in the village on the census of 1851, the year that Surrey Constabulary was formed. Soon afterwards he moved to Guildford. His Shalford home was probably Beech House (the large white house next to the Seahorse). Coincidentally, half a century later his successor Captain Sant moved into Beech House on becoming Chief Constable, and lived there from 1899 to 1904. He liked the village so much that he stayed here until his death in 1943, living on the other side of the Seahorse in The Red House (now Bahamia Court).

Shalford has always been a convenient place to live for professional men needing to be close to Guildford – lawyers, financiers, politicians, army and navy officers, and, it seems, Chief Constables. Captain Hastings and Captain Sant had only a short journey to their new County Police Station at the North Street end of Woodbridge Road (the building has recently been demolished).

Both men were from well-connected families. Captain Hastings was descended on his mother's side from Irish peers, the Viscounts Mountjoy. His father, Col. Sir Charles Holland Hastings, lost an arm at the Battle of Copenhagen in 1801. Captain Sant was the son of the artist James Sant, painter in ordinary to Queen Victoria. James Sant enjoyed a career spanning 60 years and exhibited over 300 times at the Royal Academy. He is best known for his flattering portraits of aristocratic ladies and children. Captain Sant's household at Beech House in 1901, with only three servants, was smaller than his childhood home in Lancaster Gate where his father employed six live-in servants – nurse, cook, two housemaids and a kitchen maid, a butler and a footman.

Captain Mowbray Lees Sant, 1860-1943

Surrey Constabulary was established in 1851 largely in response to an increase in burglaries, and in particular to the outrage provoked by the murder of the Vicar of Frimley in a bungled burglary. Captain Hastings retired in 1899 at the age of 86 and could look back on almost half a century during which his force had increased from just 70 men, who had to cover the whole county, to 215. The problems he had to deal with were typical of his times. They included rowdiness and disorder at the election hustings before the secret ballot was introduced by the 1872 Reform Act, and the Guildford Guy Fawkes riots of the 1850s and 1860s, when the mob lit bonfires in the streets and generally ran amok. On one occasion the County Police assisted the Guildford Police to keep order in the town, but outnumbered and in fear of their lives were forced to barricade themselves in St Mary's churchyard, while the mob broke all the windows in the County Police Station. In Dorking the police faced similar problems in trying to suppress traditional Shrove Tuesday football in the streets. The presence of the new Army Camp at Aldershot increased crime in Farnham, and the police were kept busy rounding-up deserters.

Captain Sant's problems were very much of the new century. The advent of the motor car brought rapid changes, and Captain Sant is remembered as a persecutor of motorists. He instituted police speed traps (two officers with a stop watch and tape measure), which prompted the formation of the AA. The organisation's patrolmen warned motorists of the traps, an activity challenged in a case brought by Captain Sant in 1906. (One of Captain Sant's 'victims' was Arthur Conan Doyle, caught speeding in Shalford on 20 May 1905. Challenged for doing 30 mph in a 20mph limit he said he didn't believe his car could go that fast.) Part of Captain Sant's grievance with motorists lay in the fact that cars would make criminals more mobile and increase the difficulties of the police. Criminals themselves were increasingly likely to be flashy young fellows in suits rather than the 'rough looking men' of earlier days.

But the biggest challenge of his career came with the First World War, which gave the police a key role in civil defence and hugely increased the number and range of their duties. The beginning of the war saw Captain Sant detailing groups of civilian volunteers to guard the railway line (fears of German saboteurs with sticks of dynamite), placing a police guard at Chilworth gunpowder works, and arranging 150,000 billets for troops on their way to France. Throughout the war the Chief Constable received a barrage of Home Office instructions and Defence of the Realm Regulations, all of which the police had to implement whilst their members were constantly under threat of conscription. Captain Sant's relationship with the military authorities was edgy.

He also had to make plans to receive and move on people and cattle from Sussex in the event of an invasion on the south coast, as well as arranging for the evacuation of Surrey. To assist the police four thousand Special Constables were sworn in across the county – at the top of the list was his friend the headmaster of Shalford School, Edwin Carley. For the first time the country was subject to bombing from the air. Surrey was flooded by refugees from London when air raids were expected, all needing to be housed and fed. Among the refugees were many aliens whom the police had to monitor. 'Spy mania' caused great trouble. Each report, however unlikely, had to be investigated and according to Captain Sant, 'the Public were a great nuisance.' Its

wartime role raised the status of the force, but its numbers were still not large: when Captain Sant retired in 1930 it had only 356 men.

Captain Sant devoted his remaining years to public service as a county councillor and magistrate. He was appointed Deputy Lieutenant of the county in the year he retired. Always a staunch champion of the village he had made his home he resisted proposals for street lighting and road widening that would tend

The Red House (now Bahamia Court), next to the Seahorse, and Captain Sant's home from 1904 to 1943. The house was originally called Holmdene, built in 1895 by Albert Coote.

to suburbanise the village, and strongly opposed moves by Guildford to absorb what he called 'the sentimental part of Shalford.' In vain, as in 1933 Shalford north of the Tillingbourne went into Guildford Borough and the reminder of the parish was transferred from Hambledon to Guildford Rural District.

Two Chief Constables of Surrey with very different experiences of the role. Both with Shalford connections and both are buried here: Captain Hastings rests in the churchyard with his daughter Alice, who was born in Shalford in 1851 and died aged 17 in 1868. Captain Sant was buried in 1943 in Shalford Cemetery.

Postscript: Brigadier George Roupell who won the Victoria Cross in 1915 on the western front was a son-in-law of Captain Sant. He married Doris Sant in 1921 and they later lived at Little Chartham in East Shalford Lane. During the Second World War Roupell again served in France and escaped capture by working as a farm labourer for two years before the Resistance helped him back to England. Doris Roupell was a Civil Defence volunteer in Shalford and Bramley during the war.

The name of Captain Sant's granddaughter Barbara Wace appears on the village war memorial. Aged 20 and a corporal in the Women's Auxiliary Service, she was killed in a road accident in Burma in October 1945.

Sources

Chief Constable's Reports 1851-1923 CC98/1/1-5 and Chief Constable's Report of Surrey in World War One CC98/7/; *Surrey Advertiser* reports of Captain Hastings' and Captain Sant's retirements 2 September 1899 and 20 December 1930, all at Surrey History Centre.
Pictures of Captain Hastings and Captain Sant courtesy of Surrey Police Museum

Unforgettable

' A most unforgettable person' – one former parishioner's memory of David Railton more than half a century after his brief spell as Shalford's vicar from 1931 to 1935.

Before he arrived here he was already well-known as the inspiration behind the Tomb of the Unknown Warrior in Westminster Abbey. The story has passed into legend – how as a young army chaplain on the Western Front he stood in a garden at Armentières in the silence of dusk and saw nearby a grave marked with a rough wooden cross. Pencilled on the cross were the words 'An Unknown British Soldier.' As Vicar of Margate after the war, with this image still lodged in his mind, he managed to convince the Dean of Westminster that the most fitting memorial for all who had died would be the burial of an anonymous ordinary soldier in the Abbey alongside the other national heroes. On 11 November 1920 the body of such a soldier, brought back from France with great and solemn ceremony, was laid to rest in Westminster Abbey. The Union Flag that covered the coffin was the same flag used by David Railton to cover his makeshift altar in the field of battle as he gave Holy Communion to men about to go into action, and the same flag served as a pall over their coffins as he read the burial service. It still hangs in the Abbey.

David Railton's experience amongst the soldiers at the front – marching with them footsore and exhausted, covered in mud, baked in summer and half-frozen in winter, confronting with them the sights and smells of the battlefield, trying to keep up their spirits in horrific conditions– ensured his respect for the 'Tommy' and his commitment to the welfare of ordinary people. He was embarrassed to be awarded the Military Cross having witnessed unacknowledged acts of courage and heroism by others.

He saw his great challenge after the war as rekindling enthusiasm for Christianity in the communities where he worked, using a sincere, direct and above all cheerful approach. He was a spectacularly successful preacher: queues formed outside churches where he was to preach, and at Shalford 'his sermons were wonderful…the church was always full. You had to arrive half an hour early to be sure of a seat.' He kept a watch beside him to make sure he didn't go on for too long, and never had any notes. But woe betide any choirboy heard whispering! He would be called out and made to sit in the front row, beneath the pulpit – this even happened to Railton's own son.

After Evensong David Railton led hymn singing practice - and noticed anyone who tried to sneak out after the service. 'Not that anyone wanted to. He stood on the chancel steps waving his arms, beating time, saying 'Sing up, sing up!' His favourite hymns were 'He Who Would Valiant Be' and 'Ye Holy Angels Bright.'' Likewise on Sunday School outings in a coach to Littlehampton he would lead the sing-song with traditional favourites – 'My Bonnie Lies Over the Ocean' was a certain choice.

The rousing hymn singing, upbeat approach and evangelistic fervour were a legacy from his Salvation Army parents – his father George Railton was a founder member of the movement and a close colleague of General Booth. George Railton was disappointed that his son chose not to follow him into the Salvation Army, but David Railton was instinctively seeking a way to appeal to people who would be put off both by a too-restrictive churchy approach and by the uncompromising radicalism of the Salvation Army. 'He caused a mild sensation at Shalford when he announced that hikers in shorts would be welcome in church and at services.' And unlike his teetotal Salvationist parents he could use the occasional drink to get close to his parishioners, whether joining the bellringers for a pint in the Seahorse or calling in at the British Legion for a drink and a chat with members.

He often spoke of a holiday he had spent on the road dressed as a tramp, sleeping rough, going from house to house begging 'a drop of tea for his billycan.' He experienced the kindness of some people and the unkindness of others. Of a doss house where he spent a night he said he would prefer the suspense of waiting in a front-line trench to go 'over the top' to the silent and hopeless despair of such a place.

Children were drawn to him, recognising 'a quiet, unassuming, kindly man who always had time to listen, however tired he must have been sometimes.' After his mother's death in Shalford he was touched by the sight of a little girl kneeling beside her grave in the Cemetery, and gave the child his mother's gold chain with a turquoise heart. His very practical Christianity – high ideals coupled with deep concern for the well-being of ordinary people – earned him admiration and respect. Incensed by the dreadful condition of some of the cottages in the parish he organised fund-raising to build two new houses in New Road Chilworth. At the end of his brief time in Shalford the church bells needed recasting. David Railton paid for one of the new bells himself.

He left in 1935 to become Rector of St Nicholas, Liverpool, where during the war his church was destroyed by fire. After the war he retired to Scotland, to the shores of Loch Linnhe, but was always in demand as a locum preacher. On the night of 29 June 1955, aged 70 and after a long train journey back from Sussex, he fell out of a carriage door as the train approached Fort William Station. He must have been confused in the dark and thought the train had stopped at the platform. It was a sad and incongruous end to such a life. Those he had known in Shalford spoke of being overwhelmed with sorrow on reading of his death in the newspapers the following day.

Few people are around now who have personal memories of David Railton, but his name has gone down in history. The Tomb of the Unknown Warrior is as much his memorial as that of those he wished to commemorate - in the words of its inscription, 'the many multitudes who gave the most that men can give.'

Sources: Correspondence from Mrs Betty Rowley, Mrs Phoebe Armstrong-MacDonnell and Mrs Marjorie Short. *The Times* Obituary 1 July 1955; *Surrey Advertiser* 2 July 1955; *God on Our Side: the British Padre in World War I*, by Michael Moynihan, London, 1983.
Photograph taken from the Internet – copyright unknown.

'Dear Teddy'.... A Love Story

❜ **9 September 1915**. Teddy has been in the army just a year today, hope he will be safely back before another year has gone by.
25 September. Teddy went into Action.
26 September. Teddy is missing when the roll is called.
4 October. I first receive the awful news that Teddy is missing.'

Ellen (Nellie) Dabbs in 1915

A little red notebook recently deposited at Surrey History Centre chronicles the desperate search by Nellie Dabbs for news of her fiancé, Edward (Teddy) Cutt of Peasmarsh, missing on the second day of the Battle of Loos, 26 September 1915.

Nellie Dabbs was an infant school teacher. She was six and a half years older than her 'dear Teddy'. The first pages of the little notebook list plans for her Object Lessons for the coming months: seasonal themes of flowers, fruits, animals and human activities. After Teddy disappeared she used the book to record their brief relationship and the many letters she wrote attempting to find him. A cherished only child, she lived in Broadwater near Worthing with her parents.

Nellie's family were a bit better-off than Teddy's. Her father was an ex-Naval petty officer turned market gardener, who acted as church verger and parish clerk. Teddy was the son of labourer Edward Cutt. When Teddy was small the family lived in one of four tiny four-roomed cottages on the common at Peasmarsh beside the pond. After Edward Cutt died in 1903 his widow Emily married shepherd William Childs. The new family lived at Hazel Cottage in Peasmarsh. After Teddy left school he worked as a gardener.

On the outbreak of war in 1914 volunteers rushed to enlist, including Teddy on 9 September, nine weeks before his nineteenth birthday. He was posted to the 9th Battalion of the East Surrey Regiment, based at Shoreham in Sussex, and billeted with Nellie's family at Broadwater. Her notebook records that on 30 November 1914 'Teddy first came to us so then we met for the first time.' On 2 April 1915 Teddy left Broadwater after being with them five months. The next few months of his training took place at Blackdown Camp, Redhill and Shoreham. His battalion's War Diary in the National Archives records 'Trench Warfare at Chobham Common' and no leave to be granted after 28 August in readiness for the move overseas. After he left Broadwater Nellie and Teddy spent five precious weekends at Peasmarsh, tenderly recorded in the little red book, and a whole fortnight together before he left for France. The relationship was serious and her parents came up from Sussex to meet Teddy's family.

The battalion sailed for France on 31 August. On 2 September, after a six hour march, Teddy's company slept at Avesnes: his Captain recorded 'farm buildings and cattle sheds, very dirty and little space.' They were in billets at Humbert by 5 September, and during the next fortnight practised entrenching and field attack. It can't have been very similar to their practices on Chobham Common. Unlike the Surrey heaths the French landscape was bleak, flat, coalmining country scarred with pits, waste tips and deserted miners' cottages, and already ravaged by war.

As inexperienced troops the 9th East Surreys formed part of the reserve. They became victims of a bitter rift between Field Marshall Sir John French, Commander in Chief of the British Expeditionary Force, and General Douglas Haig, commander of the First Army. French kept the raw reserves far back from the front, unwilling to use them for a heavy assault. Haig needed them on the first day of the battle, 25 September, to push through gains made in that day's fighting. The battalion's move up to the front was chaotic. Four nights of forced marches in heat and rain along roads crowded with vehicles and troops going in the opposite direction brought them to the front line near the Lens-Hulluch Road in the early hours of 26 September exhausted, hungry and thirsty. They had had nothing to eat all day as their cookers had been left behind, and had little food on the previous days. Soon after 4 am they were ordered to take cover in some captured German trenches, and even then enemy shelling prevented rations being brought to them. The delay in bringing up the reserves gave the Germans the opportunity to move in their own reserves and strengthen their barbed wire defences.

Pte Edward George Cutt

The order came to attack at 11am. As they approached the German line 1700 yards away they were cut down in swathes by shells and machine gun fire from three sides. Those who managed to reach the German barbed wire entanglements found the wire uncut and impenetrable. By 1pm the attack had failed and the order was given to retreat to the trenches they had left earlier. Enemy shelling continued all afternoon, killing many men struggling back and those that lay wounded. Teddy may have made it as far as the wire: he was seen by a wood near the German trenches, wearing his overcoat – a poignant detail. That was the last known of him. He was missing at the roll call in the evening, but there had been so much confusion, with officers lost and regiments mixed up, that for a while it seemed possible he might turn up, or at least be identified as one of the casualties. The East Surreys lost 14 officers and 438 other ranks killed or wounded, over half the strength of the battalion. Using the reserves at that stage of the battle had sacrificed them in vain.

Nellie's world fell apart when the news reached her on 4 October. Since Teddy left for France she had written to him every day. Now she wrote to the War Office, to the Red Cross in Geneva, Frankfurt and London, to the Salvation Army, to men and officers in Teddy's battalion, even to the King of Spain who tried to mediate in such cases. For a while her hopes were raised by a rumour among survivors that Teddy had been taken prisoner, but this was never substantiated. In September 1916, a year after he disappeared, the War Office concluded that unofficial reports of his death must be true. Nellie suffered a breakdown and went to stay with relatives in Grantham; her parents moved up there soon afterwards.

Ten months after Teddy disappeared Nellie was bridesmaid at her cousin's wedding. She looks very sad.

Nellie remained devoted to her Teddy and never married. She died at the age of 81 believing that Teddy had never been found. Of all the East Surreys killed on 26 September 1915 only a handful have a known grave. Most are commemorated on the Loos Memorial to the missing. But at some point Teddy's body was found. He was reburied at the end of the war in Cabaret-Rouge Cemetery at Souchez. His name is missing from the memorial tablet

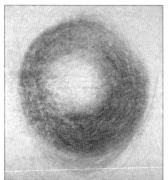

inside the parish church but appears on the war memorial on the green outside. He is listed on the memorial at St Michael's Peasmarsh.

Another poignant detail: together with the little red notebook is Teddy's copy of St John's Gospel, issued to all the troops. Inside Nellie has pinned a lock of his hair, a blond curl wrapped in a scrap of paper. This is all she had left of him. With her notebook it stands witness to the human cost of war, and to the enduring power of love.

Sources:
ESR/CUTT/25/1-8 at Surrey History Centre; WO 95/2215 War Diary of 9 Bn East Surrey Regt at the National Archives; *The History of the East Surrey Regiment* by Col H.W. Pearse and Brig Gen H.S. Sloman, published by The Medici Society Ltd., London, 1933-4, Vol. 1 pp 164-168. Photographs of Teddy and the lock of hair courtesy of Surrey History Centre. Family information and pictures of Nellie Dabbs kindly provided by Mrs Rosemary Barker and Mrs Stephanie Gash.

The Mexican Burglar

❛ Sensational sequel to alleged housebreaking at Shalford,' ran the *Surrey Advertiser's* headline: 'At Waterloo Station a man said to be a Mexican shot two detectives as they were about to arrest him.' Earlier in the day the man had committed a burglary in Pilgrims Way. But what was a Mexican doing in Pilgrims Way on the morning of 20 September 1918? Was he in fact Mexican? Did people in Shalford at that time have any idea of what a Mexican might look like? Not much, apparently.

Mrs Ede of Cyder Cottage was getting ready to take her little girl to school when she heard a knock at the door. There stood a man whose language was not too clear (but why did she assume he was Mexican?) asking if he could come in and have a wash. She agreed but told him to be quick. He washed and left, and she went out. On her return she found that he had again been in the house, and money from the child's moneybox was missing. Her neighbour Harold Gammon telephoned the police.

Today Pilgrims Way is a suburban road lined with expensive houses. In 1918 it was still a lane between fields. Cyder Cottage had been for centuries the only house there *(see map on page 13)*. Once a good yeoman's house on its own large plot it was now divided into two labourers' cottages. These were two of the poorest houses in the parish, owned by the Godwin-Austen estate and rather shabby. They had recently acquired two neighbours opposite: Chantry Edge built by Harold Gammon, a prominent Guildford draper and alderman, and The Spinney, both large, imposing properties. So this story hints at the creeping suburbanisation taking place in the early years of the twentieth century. But it says more about country life at the end of the First World War. You would allow a complete stranger to come in and have a wash in your house. You didn't lock your door when you went out. And you were so unused to foreigners that you would mistake a Canadian for a Mexican. Because it later turned out that the 'Mexican' was an AWOL Canadian soldier in civilian dress, Milfred William Grainger, aged 18, from Windsor, Ontario.

Grainger then walked to Farncombe Station where Nemesis – and the police – began to catch up with him. In the queue at the ticket office he made himself conspicuous by complaining about the price of a ticket to London (what's new?). As his train pulled out of the station a message came through with a description of the wanted 'Mexican' and the stationmaster remembered the argumentative foreigner. Two policemen were waiting at Waterloo. Grainger drew a Colt revolver and fired four shots, wounding both men, one seriously. Drama turned to farce as in a scene worthy of the Keystone Cops Grainger bolted with porters and others in hot pursuit, into a house in Lambeth Square, down the stairs, out into a yard, over an eight foot wall – then fell into the washtub of the house next door. As he attempted to climb over the next wall the owner of the washtub caught him by the leg – he pulled his revolver and she screamed and ran

Cyder Cottage photographed around the time of the First World War.
(Surrey Archaeological Society)

indoors. Two policemen and two Scottish Canadian soldiers found him hiding in the washhouse next door and captured him after a struggle.

Charged with attempted murder Grainger denied intending to shoot his victims and claimed that the gun went off by accident. Two attaché cases in his possession were found to contain a curious assortment of objects: watches, coins, a British Empire Union badge, an ammunition belt, handcuffs, metal chains, an antique pistol and an antique bayonet. These items appear to have been the fruit of earlier burglaries.

So what was the background of this young Canadian who travelled three and a half thousand miles to go on a crime spree in Surrey? Britain's declaration of war in 1914 drew Canada into the conflict and thousands of men volunteered to serve in Europe with the Canadian Expeditionary Force. A copy of Milfred Grainger's military file obtained from the Library and Archives of Canada reveals that rather than having 'Mexican' colouring he had blue eyes, light brown hair and fair skin. The *Surrey Advertiser's* description of a 'robust physique' was rather at odds with his height of 5 feet 5 inches, and a chest measurement of 34 inches. He was born on 30 November 1899 in Kingsville, Ontario, a small town on the shores of Lake Erie. His family later moved the short distance to Windsor, Canada's southernmost city, separated only by the Detroit River from Detroit USA. That part of Ontario teems with English place-names: Essex County, Norfolk, Chatham-Kent, Tilbury, Leamington, Windsor, Sandwich, London, even a River Thames. Many of the CEF had been born in Britain or had parents from Britain but a bit of online genealogical research suggests that Grainger's family had been Canadian for generations.

He enlisted on 30 March 1917 and arrived in England on 7 May. By the end of that month he was in a reserve battalion in the Canadian camp on Witley Common. He never made it to France and spent the whole of his army life at Witley – apart from the occasions when he absconded and got into trouble. The Shalford robbery was his third encounter with the law. Within six months of arriving at Witley he went on the run for a month and was sentenced to three months imprisonment with hard labour for stealing two watches from a house in Kingston. In February 1918 he received a two month prison sentence for being in unauthorised possession of a bicycle. He was AWOL again in August, his run of freedom ending with the dramatic arrest in London on 20 September.

Milfred Grainger was sentenced at the Old Bailey to five years penal servitude and committed to Wandsworth Gaol. But in July 1919 he was transferred to the Lord Derby War Hospital at Warrington for mental observation and diagnosed as 'feebleminded', a term that covered all sorts of unusual or antisocial behaviour, criminality and low IQ. He was invalided back to Canada and discharged from the army into custodial care in Windsor Ontario in September 1919.

He sounds like rather a pathetic figure: perhaps he should never have been passed fit for the army in the first place. For all its elements of melodrama and mistaken identity, in the end the story of the Mexican Burglar in Pilgrims Way is a sad one – not least for the policemen he shot but also for Milfred Grainger himself. And as a postscript, despite his behaviour, the Canadian authorities decided that he was entitled to the British War Medal for his service overseas.

Sources:
Surrey Advertiser 21, 23, 25 September, 5 October, 16 December 1918.
Library and Archives of Canada: military file of Milfred William Grainger, regimental number 2042558.

Broadford

For centuries nothing stirred at Broadford except waterfowl on the flooded meadows and the occasional horse and cart splashing through the wide shallow ford. That changed after the river Wey was made navigable to Godalming in 1764. New industry grew up on the river – at first wharves and timber yards, later mills and a brewery. River traffic increased after 1816 when the new Wey and Arun Canal joined with the Godalming Navigation near Stonebridge wharf.

At first the river at Broadford was just dredged deeper for barges, and owners of carts wishing to take them through the ford had to apply in advance to have the water lowered. The problems this caused led to a bridge being built in 1808. Broadford became a little industrial hamlet. The two or three cottage plots sandwiched between the Common and the river became increasingly developed with industry and houses inhabited by workers in the new industries.

Labourers, sawyers, coopers, engineers and clerks worked at the brewery established at Broadford by William Parsons in 1845 and expanded by Frederick Webb after 1863. Parsons bought several houses at Broadford to accommodate his employees. The Brewery was sold to Savills Brewery of Godalming in 1891. The Parrot originated as an offshoot of the brewery and is Shalford's oldest surviving pub after the Seahorse. The site occupied by the brewery, the

The Parrot was originally an offshoot of William Parsons' Broadford Brewery

Parrot and Broadford House used to be part of a millwright's and blacksmith's premises. Millwright Richard Clark bought land there in 1825; Charles Harris followed him as millwright and was living at Broadford House prior to 1866. The sluice gates beside the wheel at Elstead Mill are marked with the name 'Harris Shalford 1842.' Beyond Broadford House lay Stonebridge wharf and a field beside it where timber was piled awaiting shipment by barge. Gunpowder from the Chilworth mills was kept in a special storehouse that still survives at the wharf.

Broadford Brewery operated from 1845 until 1913. The works centred on a cobbled courtyard whose buildings were topped by a distinctive landmark – a tall wooden turret with a weather vane consisting of a barrel and malt shovel and other brewing implements. In 1916 the vacant premises were acquired by the Godalming Sanitary Laundry and converted to a steam laundry, washing army uniforms day and night. Each week 80,000 items from nearby army camps arrived in truckloads at Shalford

Station. Most of the hundred employees were women, but the manager, William Pullinger, was spared military service because his work was regarded as so crucial. After the war the laundry was employed solely in cleaning army uniforms and bedding.

(Courtesy of Colin Jelley whose mother Florence Young worked at the laundry 1917-18)

One August night in 1923 the premises spectacularly burnt down in a blaze so fierce that from Guildford it seemed that half Godalming must be on fire. The wooden turret fell swiftly into flames that rapidly engulfed the rest of the buildings. It was fortunate for the night shift that they were on their tea break or their escape would have been cut off. Broadford Cottage and the Parrot were in danger, as were the houses on the other side of the road with a fierce wind blowing sparks in their direction. The Common was soon covered with furniture hurriedly brought out of the houses and from the Parrot and Broadford Cottage, home of the Laundry manager, Captain Mitchell. Piles of army blankets lay around, salvaged from the burning laundry. The Guildford and Godalming fire brigades brought the blaze under control; it was still smouldering the following afternoon – the works almost completely destroyed.

Four years later the derelict premises were purchased by Mr A. Filmer Jacobs, the founder of Vulcanised Fibre Ltd. In 1930 the company also acquired the lease of Stonebridge Meadow and Wharf beside the works and expanded production over the

whole of that site. 'Vulcanised fibre' consisted of compressed layers of specially treated paper produced in sheets or tubes and 'as light as aluminium, as tough as horn and as hard as leather.' It made containers such as suitcases and components for electrical and mechanical industries. Vulcanised Fibre was a big employer of local people – by 1936 the workforce numbered 150 – but it was also a noisy

Broadford in the autumn floods of 1950
(courtesy of Surrey History Centre)

neighbour. In 1929 Broadford residents complained to the parish council that noise from the works at night made it impossible to sleep except on Saturdays. Sheets being released from the drying room were to blame. The firm promised to try to abate the noise but more complaints followed.

During the Second World War the Broadford works again served the war effort. Vulcanised fibre was used to make jettisonable extra fuel tanks for fighter aircraft, including the Spitfire. The firm's publicity posters of the time capture national pride in the Spitfire, allied to their own product. During the war the fibre works had its own ARP patrol and its own platoon of Home Guard. The works siren warned of air raids. Many of the workforce were now women, the men away on active service.

In 1967 the firm merged with Spaulding Fibre and became known as Spaulding Russell. The firm struggled to survive the recession of the 1970s and the Broadford works finally closed in 1982. Its tall chimney, by now a familiar landmark, was demolished a few years later. The phoenix that rose from the ashes was the new Broadford Park. Broadford House remains alongside new glass-fronted buildings which reflect sky, clouds and foliage, echoing the water of the river and the often-flooded meadows. This design received the Guildford Society's Best New Building award in 1987.

The tall chimney of the Vulcanised Fibre works reflected in the 1968 floods (courtesy of Frances Grey)

Gone are the wharves and barges laden with timber or gunpowder. Gone are the blacksmiths, the millwrights, the sawyers and coopers, the brewers, the steam laundry and the fibre works. In their place have come modern communications technologies, specialists in IT and computer software, design consultants, and designers of components for racing cars. Pleasure boats moor below the bridge and wharf, and a continuous stream of traffic crosses the bridge across the Wey. Road and river form part of an ever-changing landscape, constantly evolving to meet new social and economic needs.

Sources
Surrey Advertiser 18 August 1923; Records of Vulcanised Fibre ref 1765 (photographs boxes 15 and 16); Shalford Parish Council Minutes ref P66/1/5 and 6: all at Surrey History Centre.
The Breweries and Public Houses of Guildford Part Two, 1995, Mark Sturley
The Wey Navigations An Historical Guide, Alan R Wardle, 2003

In a Vicarage Garden

It's surprising what stories gardens can tell. The garden of Shalford's former vicarage has seen a few changes over the centuries. The house was sold off by the Church in 1948; at that time it was considered too large and the upkeep too costly. It is now divided into two: The Old Vicarage and Bridge House.

A few years ago a garden historian contacted me about a garden plan for a 'Mrs Bartlemew' at Shalford drawn by landscape gardener Joseph Spence in 1762. I was able to confirm that this must be the vicarage garden, as Charles Bartholmew was vicar from 1762 to 1800 (Shalford's longest serving vicar, in fact). The plan, on microfilm at Surrey History Centre, came as a delight and a revelation. The garden plan included the rear part of the house. This showed the vicarage as it was before the Victorian alteration and enlargement (the present building) and even before an earlier alteration in 1798. Shalford's vicarage seems to have been a typical medieval house with a central hall and two wings – not particularly large. It might even have been a hall house enlarged in the Tudor period. It lay further back from the road than the present house, which was extended forward during the Victorian alterations.

The garden plan reveals the eighteenth century fashion for incorporating 'romantic' vistas into garden design. Formal flower beds, gravel paths, lawns and specimen trees worked with and framed views from the parlour windows: immediately to the west 'the Vale with the Navigable River,' to the north west 'the ruin on Caterine Hill,' (the local pronunciation) and to the south 'the road, a rising lawn, and wooded lontananza.'

'Wooded lontananza' – how lovely. This must mean a distant view. There is no view now: the trees have grown up, not only on the boundary of the garden itself but also in the landscape beyond. The romantic ruin of St Catherine's chapel was also used as a ready-made folly by the owner of nearby Shalford House, Robert Austen, who 'improved' it to enhance the view from his dining room. From St Catherine's Hill today both the site of Shalford House and the vicarage are no longer visible.

The life of an eighteenth century vicar of Shalford seems to have been idyllic. Apparently a great cricketer in his youth, in later life Charles Bartholmew was better known as a poet, and published a few 'slight'

The Georgian vicarage,
renovated in 1798, drawn
by John Hassell in 1822

pieces. He composed a version of the *Iliad*, and was fond of reciting passages to friends and neighbours. Gazing out of his parlour window he saw not the wooded lontananza of Surrey and villagers trudging along the dusty road into Guildford, but Hector and Achilles and the distant towers of Troy. He may have had little to do with the poorer people of the parish, most of whom didn't attend church anyway. He was not a rich man and in 1756 and 1769 he applied, unsuccessfully, for the post of Master of the Royal Grammar School in Guildford. This would have left even less time for parish duties. His successor as vicar of Shalford was George Walton Onslow who held other livings as vicar of Send and rector of Wisley, and entrusted Shalford and Bramley to his curate, Henry Knowles Creed, who lived at the vicarage.

Half a century later the church and the vicar played a much more active role in the parish. Richard Browne Matthews, vicar from 1855 – 1885, had the vicarage greatly enlarged – look for his initials 'RBM' above the door to Bridge House (except when driving round that dangerous bend!). The new house was one of the largest in the parish and its size emphasised the authority of the church; it also had a waiting room for the poor who wanted to consult the vicar about their problems. For twenty-five years Richard Browne Matthews managed the village school, established in 1855 specifically to educate the children of the labouring classes in the principles of the church (with sewing and the 3Rs as well). He was a founder of and frequent performer at the Penny Readings at the Shalford Institute, educational entertainment affordable to all.

What happened to Mrs Bartholmew's garden after the vicarage was rebuilt? Instead of the carefully sited elms and cherry trees, and the lilac hedge, a screen of conifers encloses the garden. The gravel paths and flower beds are laid to lawn, smooth enough to indulge the Victorian passion for croquet. There is actually a pictorial record of a game of croquet in the Vicarage garden. In 1894 the vicar, Hugh Huleatt, let the house for the summer while he went on holiday. It was rented by the aunts of the artist E.H. Shepard (illustrator for *Punch* and *Winnie the Pooh*). He and his brother stayed with the aunts: 'We had a grand holiday.' The grown-ups played croquet on the Vicarage lawn. One day Aunt Emily took 'a mighty swipe at the ball and we watched, horrified, as the ball bounded across the lawn straight for the legs of the curate...The ball caught him fair and square and with a loud squawk he leapt into the air.' The illustration (*right*) appears in his autobiography, *Drawn from Life*. Also note in the picture a trestle table with glasses and a jug – home-made lemonade, without a doubt. And the uniformed maidservant pouring it out: on

the 1891 census the vicar had four live-in servants: sewing maid, cook, housemaid and parlourmaid.

The Victorian vicarage built in 1856 and 1865, now The Old Vicarage and Bridge House

Fifty years on and the vicarage garden had assumed a more sinister aspect. It found itself on the GHQ Stopline, the line of defences intended to impede a German advance towards London. A shellproof pillbox was built in the garden to cover the crossing of the Tillingbourne – one of several pillboxes along the Tillingbourne and East Shalford Lane. With the roadblock at the Seahorse the stage was set for what might have been one of the biggest battles of the war.

But all things pass. The pillbox, mossy and surrounded by greenery in the garden of Bridge House, has more recently served as a wendy house, toolshed, and garden feature. A clematis is trained round the entrance. The story told by the vicarage garden is the story not only of the vicarage itself but of changes that have taken place in the history of the village and the nation, just as much as any house or family history.

The shellproof pillbox in the garden of Bridge House, covering the crossing of the main road over the Tillingbourne

With thanks to Mrs and Mrs Dewdney of The Old Vicarage, and Mr and Mrs Wolfenden of Bridge House.

Sources: Illustration from *Drawn from Life* by E.H. Shepard, Methuen, 1962, © The Estate of E.H. Shepard, reproduced with permission of Curtis Brown Group Ltd., London. Joseph Spence's garden plan on microfilm at Surrey History Centre ref Z/312/1/1. 'Shalford Parsonage, 1822', by J. Hassell reproduced by kind permission of Surrey History Centre.

Shalford's Pillboxes

As the threat of invasion loomed in the summer of 1940 thousands of pillboxes were hastily constructed across the country, beside rivers and lanes, in gardens, fields and hedgerows. Twenty thousand were built nationwide, two thousand in Surrey.

Shalford has around a dozen remaining. Most are a reticent presence, barely visible under brambles and greenery. Aerial views such as Google Earth sometimes show a small grey curve peeking out from a mass of vegetation. Some have been demolished for new development. Others are neglected and vandalised, (one by the Wey at Farncombe is covered with graffiti and surrounded by rubbish). A few have fallen victim to human aesthetic sense. The box in the garden of Whistlers Corner at the end of Tilehouse Road took a month to demolish in 2007. Built to withstand the guns of the German army it fell after valiant resistance to the pneumatic drills. It had even survived an air raid on 8 October 1940, when a bomb fell across the road just yards away.

The pillboxes were constructed as part of the GHQ Stopline, a line of defences intended to halt or delay a German advance on London. Guildford was designated a Nodal Point, where a concerted effort would have been made to stop the enemy passing through. The German 9th Army after landing in Sussex would have confronted the Stopline at Shalford, a natural defensive point formed by the convergence of the Wey and the Tillingbourne at the Guildford Gap. The Tillingbourne was in effect an anti-tank ditch fortified by pillboxes along its northern bank.

On the main road through the village the Seahorse featured in the plans as a 'defended locality'. Beside the wall one of the three concrete pillars of the roadblock remains, with its slot for a steel barrier. A pillbox was built into the garden bank, and loopholes for rifles were cut into the west and south walls of the pub. A wide anti-tank ditch from the Wey crossed Dagley Lane and extended across the pub's garden: the Seahorse's strawberry bed fell victim to the war. Concrete blocks were placed over the yard. Another anti-tank ditch was dug near the Mill. There was even a plan – never put into effect - to flood the Tillingbourne valley to a width of 300 feet by damming the river upstream of the Mill.

The building contractors for the Shalford works were John Mowlem & Co, who had a temporary office and workshop by the Scout hut. Mowlem's engineer was Fred Bowman, who married Phyllis Smith, the daughter of the Seahorse's landlord, in 1942. In 1990 he recorded useful and fascinating memories of constructing pillboxes and other defence works between Farncombe and Chilworth Manor – twenty-seven pillboxes were built across this stretch of country. In most cases Mowlems did not use the Army's standard hexagonal designs, but opted for a circular structure twenty feet in diameter. Each pillbox had 65 cubic yards of concrete in the walls, with a concrete base and fifteen inches of concrete and reinforced steel in the roof. The total weight

was in the region of 119 tons. No wonder the Whistlers Corner box was able to withstand the drills for so long. Some boxes were of heavier construction and designated as shellproof. Shellproof pillboxes include the one in the garden of Bridge House (*see page 66*), covering the crossing of the Tillingbourne on the main road, and the pillboxes along the Wey.

The pillbox at Kingfishers in East Shalford Lane overlooks a wide stretch of the Tillingbourne

The pillboxes were not designed to stand exposed in all their grey nakedness. They were camouflaged, often ingeniously dressed with painted boards to look like cottages or agricultural buildings. One at Albury appeared as a very convincing petrol station, complete with pump. At Farncombe beside the Wey a pillbox was disguised as a bathing hut. In the countryside many were deliberately placed under trees and in copses to escape detection from the air, and covered with a 'natural' camouflage of greenery woven into netting. Surviving pillboxes have been turned to a variety of uses. The one at Kingfishers (*above*) served as a boys' den. Others have been decorated with paint or trellis or used as a garden shed. Bats like their cave-like cool darkness, so some have become dedicated bat roosts.

The disguises belied the pillboxes' deadly purpose. The weapons to be deployed in each were rifles and a Bren gun (a light machine gun). The box guarding the bridge over the Tillingbourne at East Shalford (*left*) has a larger opening for an anti-tank gun. The 4th Battalion of the Surrey Home Guard manned the Tillingbourne pillboxes, but if the invasion had gone ahead Canadian and Reserve divisions would have reinforced the Home Guard at the Stopline. There was to be no retreat: the Home Guard were instructed to fight to the last man and the last bullet. Men would have died in these pillboxes,

Spot the pillbox. Submerged in vegetation, still guarding the bridge on East Shalford Lane.

defending families, homes and country against the invader. This was the biggest threat since Napoleon's army was camped within sight of the cliffs of Dover. The Battle of Shalford could have been one of the biggest battles of the war.

The RAF and the Navy saved the nation. Britain's command of the skies and seas forced Hitler to abandon the invasion plans. Defensive strategy changed and the pillboxes became redundant. Like the other defence works of the war they were never intended to linger in the landscape. The anti-tank ditches were filled in soon after the war, but the obdurate concrete of the pillboxes often meant that it was easier to leave them be than remove them. Now they form another layer in the archaeological record, part of the historic landscape. Their emotional resonance is heightened by their role in a conflict that is still part of many people's personal experience. But few pillboxes have protected status – none of those in Surrey are listed. The pillboxes' best hope lies in communities appreciating their significance. Don't these unassuming monuments to Britain's finest hour deserve our respect?

Sources
'The Last Stand Against Hitler might have been outside the Seahorse', Matthew Alexander in the *Surrey Advertiser* 31 August 1990; *Guildford, The War Years*, David Rose and Graham Collyer, 1999; *The GHQ Line: pillbox defence line of 1940*, C. Alexander, 1993 (unpublished, at Surrey History Centre). All these include Fred Bowman's reminiscences.
Records relating to Local Defence Volunteers and Home Guard ref 477 at Surrey History Centre – includes maps with defence structures marked.
Captured German version of OS Map of SW Surrey with some defensive installations marked, ref 6669/2 at Surrey History Centre.
http://www.pillbox-study-group.org.uk; Wikipedia: British Hardened Field Defences of World War II. Both accessed 21 Jan 2008
Invasion! Operation Sealion 1940, by Martin Marix Evans, 2004
Twentieth Century Military Sites, English Heritage, 2003
The Kingfishers pillbox photographed thanks to Andrea Campion-Smith

The Seahorse roadblock: one concrete pillar remains with a slot for the barrier

Archives:
Surrey History Centre 130 Goldsworth Road Woking GU21 6ND
The National Archives Ruskin Avenue Kew Richmond TW9 4DU
London Metropolitan Archives 40 Northampton Road London EC1R 0HB